Welcome to the wonderfu
this book was born years ago when there were few sources for what modern authors were looking for: descriptive phrases that related to today's ever-changing contemporary market. Similarly, I'd not found anything to help with historical writing.

After much deliberation, I decided I needed to come up with a compendium of tags for those of us who write historical fiction. I'd already started my own list of historical tags and simply began to expand on it.

Whether your passion is to write a novel, an article for a newspaper or magazine, or to write a blog, as you know, it can be a challenge to come up with the right combination of words to leave your audience wanting to come back for more. Every day new books are uploaded to the web. How do you get today's readers to choose your book? By creating settings they can see, characters they can care about, storylines they want to read more of. None of that is easy, but that's where *The Historical Phrase Book – Regency-Medieval Edition* comes into play. (There is also a second volume, *The Historical Phrase Book – Western-Viking Edition.*)

There are only so many words in the English language. How you use and arrange those words sets you apart from other writers.

When you're sitting at your computer staring at an empty screen because what you want to say next simply won't come to mind, that's the time to open *The Historical Phrase Book – Regency-Medieval Edition* to jog your senses. Not to copy the tags from this book. That's too simple. Read the descriptors and let your imagination run wild—and you'll come up with that perfect scene that has eluded you.

Some tags/phrases are universal no matter the venue, but the right combination can do so much more than merely describe. As a publisher and editor, I cringe when I read 'He smiled.' There is so much more depth that can be revealed. Make your reader *see* that smile, *feel* the emotion behind it. The right choice of words can set the tone, bring the setting to life, establish point of view, tighten the suspense or add emotion.

One thing I learned while compiling these descriptors is that many overlap, so don't limit yourself to just one section. Take the Regency period. The descriptors not only fit those living in

England, but also the wealthy who came across the pond to the United States and wanted to emulate the lifestyle of the *ton*. Short of putting the tags in every section where they could possibly be used—which would have probably tripled the size of this book—I put them where they fit the best. So don't limit yourself. Check out multiple sections. The size of the book also necessitated having two volumes. The second volume in this series is *The Historical Phrase Book – Western-Viking Edition.*

As I mentioned before, the purpose of *The Historical Phrase Book – Regency-Medieval Edition* isn't for you to copy these phrases into your work. It's designed to be a valuable, beneficial, inspiring writer's tool. The tags found between these pages are here to entice your imagination so you may create your own rich descriptions. Used to prod your thought process, there is no limit to what *you* can create. Where there is blank space in this book, write in your own tags.

In *The Historical Phrase Book – Regency-Medieval Edition* I have included numerous categories, including some historical facts. And I would be remiss to not include a romance section. Write clean/Christian fiction? No problem at all. So do I. This book has been set up to address that issue. Just ignore the 'lovemaking' section. For those authors that write spicier, feel free to avail yourself of that section.

I hope you enjoy *The Historical Phrase Book – Regency-Medieval Edition* and use this resource to spark your creativity, inspire your imagination, and kick your muse into gear. This is your tool—use it to your advantage. If you write multiple categories like I do, I hope you will also check out *The Historical Phrase Book – Western-Viking Edition.* Tags in it are completely different than in this book and there are multiple categories that are different as well.

Enjoy!

Leanne

The Historical Phrase Book

Regency ~ Medieval Edition

Leanne Burroughs

Highland Press Publishing
Florida

The Historical Phrase Book

Regency-Medieval Edition

For information, please contact
Highland Press Publishing,
PO Box 2292, High Springs, FL 32655.
www.highlandpress.org

Print ISBN: 978-1-942606-21-5

Highland Press Publishing

http://highlandpress.org

Reference

Table of Contents

Dedication

To my husband, Tom. Because of your extended hospitalization, last year was one of our worst, but God was with you every step of the way and you came through it and I'm praising Him for that. We just celebrated our 48th wedding anniversary. Here's to 48 more.

I love you!

1

ENGLAND ~ REGENCY ~ VICTORIAN ~ GEORGIAN ~ EDWARDIAN

A. Time Periods

*~

Edwardian Period ~ 1901-1910

Georgian Period ~ 1714-1830 (1837 if you go to the end of William IV's reign)

Regency Period ~ 1811-1820

Victorian Period ~ 1837-1901

B. Rankings/Status

*~

a bastard of a noble man? Hate rose within him

a landed noble

a landless second brother

a simple country squire

a title holder could (but rarely did) marry beneath him. Younger aristocratic sons could be cut off completely if they married a woman from the lower classes

aristocrats wed other aristocrats or persons who shared their social standing

baron/baroness ~ lowest of the five peerage ranks

Baronet ~ title of the first rank below the peerage, but above a knight; a hereditary title, considered a member of the gentry, not nobility, addressed as 'Sir First name' and his wife as 'Lady last name'

Beau Monde ~ (French for 'beautiful world', pronounced bo mɔ̃d) and *polite society* have been interchangeable with *le bon ton* during the nineteenth century

Burt's peerage ~ book

Debrett's Peerage & Baronetage ~ since 1789, Debrett's is an annually published guide to the peerage; also called the 'Society Book'

dowager ~ widow of a Peer of the Realm; the term isn't typically applied unless the new titled Peer has a wife

duke/duchess ~ highest rank of the nobility; always addressed as 'Your Grace' or 'Duke;' hereditary title

earl/countess ~ third highest rank of the nobility; a hereditary title connected to an area, as in Earl of *wherever*

English peerage runs according to primogeniture—for example, the eldest son gets almost everything. If a peer has no eldest son, the title and possessions that belong to it go to the next male heir, usually a brother or nephew

feel concerned, not threatened. I've heard he may be the bastard son of...

gentleman ~ someone who does not have to work for a living; could be introduced to ladies at a ball solely for the purpose of dancing, but couldn't presume to further the acquaintance afterward

gentry ~ class of country landowners just below the aristocrats, such as baronets, knights, and non-titled squires. Often rented out their properties. Unlike aristocrats above them, they didn't always migrate to London for the Season each year, often tending to stay in the country

heir to an earldom

knight ~ lowest rank within the gentry, a non-hereditary title, not of the peerage

looked every inch the country gentleman

marquess/marquis ~ pronounced markwess)/marchioness (pronounced marshuness) ~ second highest rank within the peerage–just below a duke and above an earl, typically holds secondary titles

members of the *ton* came from the aristocracy, the gentry, royalty and monarchs. Though some wealthier members of the middle classes might have married into the lower ranks of the gentry, such unions wouldn't have been completely accepted by the elite *ton*

middle class ~ better off than 'working class', but not rich; genteel professions such as barristers, clergy, high level scholars, physicians (not surgeons), politicians, and professors. These professions were open to gentlemen who had enough money to not *have* to work, but who wanted to do something meaningful with their time

most peers do not use their surnames as their title

nob ~ a person of wealth or social standing

no one below the rank of Earl or chief could own a deerhound

nobility ~ class of people of high rank or birth

noble in appearance and bearing

one of a rank worthy of her father's

only a third son, though he's not without means

Peer of the Realm ~ nobleman with a hereditary seat in the House of Lords: Duke, Marquess, Earl, Viscount, or Baron

peers automatically had seats in the House of Lords

primogeniture ~ traditional system of inheritance – eldest male offspring was the sole recipient of the deceased's title and entailed lands. Money, possessions, and non-entailed properties could be divided up among children of the deceased, but dispensations to younger sons and daughters were typically modest

Prinny ~ nickname for the Prince Regent

rich, titled, and *attractive/handsome*, he

royalty were forgiven any transgression. Scandalous activities such as having illegitimate children or conducting extra-marital affairs incited gossip, but were typically overlooked for members of the aristocracy. Such conduct among the gentry, however, could destroy an entire family's social aspirations

social ladder ~ *ton* society was intensely class-conscious and the social hierarchy was incredibly rigid. Birth, wealth, titles, and other factors determined class standing: Monarch, Royalty, Aristocracy, Gentry, Middle Classes, Artisans & Trades people, Servants, Laboring Poor, Paupers

social positions could be altered or determined by income, houses, speech, clothing, or even manners. Climbing the social ladder could take generations, particularly into the aristocracy who didn't readily accept those of inferior birth into their ranks

the haughty, preening aristocrat

the life of a coddled noble

the Regency wasn't the era of arranged marriages, unless it was members of the Royal Family. However, royals whose marriages were arranged participated in the selection and rejection of proposed suitors. English royals typically married those born to other Protestant European royal families

ton ~ high society; pronounced tone

ton has also been used as an interchangeable term with the Upper Ten Thousand of later 19th century society, including most of the peerage, aristocracy and the wealthy merchants or bankers of the City (London)

t*on* is a term used to refer to Britain's high society during the late Regency and reign of George IV, and later. During the eighteenth century, it was borrowed from the French word meaning 'taste' or 'the highest style.' The full phrase is *le bon ton*, meaning good manners or 'in the fashionable mode'–characteristics held as ideal by the British *beau monde*

viscount (pronounced vycount)/viscountess

C. Dwellings

*~

an ancestral estate that would go to his older brother

as the group made their way to the dining room bedchamber

bounded up the stairs, taking the steps two at a time

cloaked in the gloom of the darkened balcony, he

dower house ~ typically a small house on an estate to which the dowager could retire when the new heir took up residence

drawing room/parlor/salon ~ formal room for receiving visitors, and the chamber where the ladies would withdraw to have tea after dinner while the men stayed at the table socializing or retired to the game room

dropped into a window seat

dual ornately carved staircases rose to

from the white-painted wainscoting to the elegant crown molding

glancing around the quiet, lamplit library

have all gone to the country for shooting season

he wished he could deny it, but the truth was, after having moved to the earl's townhouse, *whoever* found himself missing *whoever* at dinner

high ceilinged

his magnificent country seat

his townhouse overlooked Grosvenor Square

home ~ condition of domesticity, or one's permanent and regular shelter, but not the physical structure or property

house was large and imposing

huddled beside a blazing fire

huge oaken doors swung wide

King Street ~ a row of tidy townhouses

large wrap-around porch, two-story bay windows, and third story turret

mid-summer migrations to their stately houses country house ~ a mansion in the countryside. The more ostentatious a person could make it, the bigger the status symbol. Country houses typically have huge landscape gardens

moved through the shadowy depths of the house

nursery ~ located out of earshot on the top floor of a residence, the nursery had children's beds, furniture, play area, and schoolroom area and areas for the *nurses/governesses*

paced his study in a determined manner

parlour ~ reception room

pausing at the stairs, *his/her* hand on the newel post, *he/she*

quincy ~ indoor toilet

received her in her private sitting room

terrace ~ row of identical or mirror-image houses sharing side walls, i.e. townhouses

the ancestral home of

the house would be swollen with guests by nightfall

the very heart of Bond Street, where all the *beau monde* assembled to adorn their debutantes and their dandies

their estates bordered each other

townhouse ~ historically, residence of a peer or member of the aristocracy in the capital or major city

traveling from one grand estate to the next

vaulted ceilings

Victorian home with gracious fine china, parlours and paintings

you might retire to one of the less fashionable houses and live quietly

D. Furnishings/Fixtures

*~

a cheery fire burned

a dainty piecrust table by her chair

a goosefeather mattress in the chamber

a log sparked

a long branch beating a rhythmic cadence against the room

a porte cochere arched over them

an elaborate chandelier cast a soft glow on the arriving guests

and the finest and handsomest table

Aubusson carpet

bath chair ~ wheelchair

bed was made of stripped pine logs

brick walkways

bright rag rugs covered

cart or wheeled stand used for conveying something (as food or books) ('a supermarket trolley'; 'a tea trolley'), i.e. cart/wagon

carved stair rails

casket ~ a small box, especially for antique jewels

chimney pot ~ smoke-stack atop a house. But refers to the cylindrical topmost part. The part below is the chimney or chimney stack

closet ~ a small room, i.e. water closet

colorful throws rested over the furniture

counterpane ~ like a bedspread, blanket

coverlid ~ bed-quilt, counterpane

creamware bowl ~ Cream-coloured earthenware produced chiefly from 1750 to 1820

curtains swayed from the gentle breeze through the open window

detailed gazebos

epergne ~ large, ornate, often silver table centerpiece with multiple tiers that held dishes, candles and a large urn of soup. It was the tallest piece in the center of the table

escritoire ~ small writing desk with a sloping front door hinged at the bottom edge that could be opened down to provide a writing area. Interior often contained small drawers and compartments designed to hold things such as an ink pot, sand container, blotter, and writing feathers or pens

first floor ~ floor above ground level

folly ~ an ornamental building in a garden

foolscap ~ writing paper, often imprinted with a watermark of a jester's cap

however many stories of mullioned windows

lacelike plasterwork on the ceiling

lavatory ~ toilet

longcase clock ~ grandfather or grandmother clock

loveseat ~ a seat which accommodates two people facing in opposite directions. Can be wooden or padded

men and women had separate sleeping quarters

nécessaire ~ a small bag or case for cosmetics/jewellery

orangery ~ greenhouse or conservatory— where fruits such as lemons, oranges, pineapples, as well as decorative greenery were grown in a 'winter' garden

ornate Baroque-styled chair

perched on the settle ~ a wooden bench, usually with arms and a high back, long enough to accommodate three or four sitters

pier glass mirror

pillar box ~ the bright red mail box

pram/perambulator ~ baby carriage

sweeping green lawns dotted here and there by ash trees

the ceiling decorated with trefoils and medallions

the *inside a mixture of leather and wood/longcase clock struck*

the newly placed glass windows rattled in their panes

three huge crystal chandeliers hung from the wooden cross-beamed ceiling, each filled with dozens of beeswax candles

toilet ~ room containing the toilet, not the actual commode itself

walls were lit by morning light from a large oval window

WC ~ water closet

whatever color silk bed with curtains

E. Actions/Activities

*~

a short stroll along the Serpentine ~ Hyde Park

a small boat ferried passengers across the Thames

admitting her to a place within their ranks

advanced until they stood toe-to-toe. *Whoever* refused to give him the satisfaction of backing up, much less flinching

after morning riding came breakfast. Ladies went shopping or took care of household chores, i.e. paying bills. They only made morning calls on those they knew extremely well. A well-bred person didn't call on casual acquaintances in the morning. After lunch, men went to Parliament or the club. Ladies paid more calls, filling the hours between 12:00 p.m. and 5:00 p.m. Calls shouldn't exceed 1/2 hour in length–10 to 20 minutes was considered adequate. If others arrived while paying a call, it was considered polite for the first caller to politely leave

after wiping his lips with his serviette

almost knocked him off his pins ~ legs

as he stropped the razor

asked for her hand and was summarily dismissed

attended by a clutch of young swains

bedlam reigned

before I shackle myself to some fishwife or milksop

befouled his plans

began her morning toilette

being measured in a little mantua maker's shop

blew her nose in a most unladylike fashion

brandishing swords

brushed her cheek with warm fingers

brushed his *knuckles lightly against her cheeks/thumbs over her cheekbones*

brushing his knuckles affectionately *over/across* her cheeks

bustled into the drawing room caressed her skin with his knuckles

caressed his stubbled cheek

carry on gentlemen ~ continue

caught her hand in his, brought it to his lips

caught within the circle of his arms, she tipped back her head to look up at him

cease your missishness

chafed against Society's rules for young ladies

combed all the Society haunts, from Bond Street to Hyde Park, from the opera to the theatre

considered penning a note and sending her regrets

conspicuously silent about

could still feel his lips upon hers

couldn't *believe his cheeky behavior/ignore the strictures of his class/recall being so fuddled*

cradled in his arms, she lost all rational thought

cupped his stubbled cheeks in her palms

cursed his current straights ~ conditions/situation

dabbed at her nose with a handkerchief she'd retrieved from her sleeve

dallying with anyone in skirts

debutante ~ upon completing her education and being polished with social graces, a young girl–around seventeen–would be presented to Society by her parents or guardians. Also called her *coming-out*. For the elite of Regency London, the first official event for young ladies who came out each year was to be presented to the ruling monarch and the Court. After that, their parents usually threw a lavish debut ball, making sure to invite the most eligible young bachelors of the *ton*

deemed him acceptable for their now 37-year-old maiden daughter. He, therefore, fled to her

Derby and The Oaks ~ (pronounced dar-bee) the two major horse races in England, held at Epson Downs, Surrey in late May or early June

did he give you leave to use his Christian name

didn't wish to draw undue attention

discussing the delicious on-dits concerning

doing her best to lure you to the parson's noose

doing it much too brown ~ over-doing it, not credible

don't *get yourself into a taking/take a pet, m'dear*

doomed to spinsterhood (after three unsuccessful seasons)

draining his carefully allotted racing purse

dreaded that he might cast up his accounts right there in your ballroom

drew her like a moth to a flame

drew out his snuff box and took a pinch

drew his knuckles gently over his cheek

drove himself hell for leather

duel ~ by the Regency period pistols were more frequently used than swords as a means of settling disputes of honor. When a challenge had been issued, the offending person could apologize, but if he chose not to, then he and his opponent would meet on a 'field of honor.' Dueling by now was actually illegal, but it was rarely prosecuted since it was the privileged who usually challenged someone. Seconds worked out the where and when. A surgeon's presence gave medical care to the wounded

dueling doesn't pleasure me the way it does you

eagerly opened the missive

encouraged to have no opinions at all (women)

extending his arm, she placed her hand in the crook of his elbow

face heated from embarrassment

fancies himself very much the man about town

feather-light, his finger grazed her cheek

fell tail over teakettle down the hill ~ i.e. head over heels

felt a bit out of curl ~ not quite right, i.e. a fellow gets a bit out of curl in weather like this

felt *a moment of victory when she didn't pull away/an odd stab of jealousy*

felt an uncontrollable need to lean against *whoever's* chest and feel the security of his arms enfold her

felt the soft scratch of his whiskers against her face

for some reason the woman felt she had a duty to insinuate herself into her life and instruct her on all matters to do with propriety

formal dinners, fancy balls, soirees, musicales, rides through Hyde Park, London townhouses, country manors

found himself fed, wined and wenched to his satisfaction

found it handsomely appointed

freed his sword

gave a smug smile before informing the butler to allow Lord *whomeve*r entry

gave him the mitten ~ broke up

give the poor chap

grinding/ground his *cheroot/cigar* hard beneath his bootheel

grinned like a child with a new toy as he drove the curricle down Park Lane

had been *an addlepate to believe/want-witted enough to purchase*

had been *bird-witted to embark upon/possessed of few friends in London*

had fair knocked him senseless ~ almost

had he *gone queer in the attic to/pockets to let*

had *her in a fine fettle/ruffled her English sensibilities again*

had two households completely in sixes and sevens

hadn't paid much heed to her when

hands were gentle as he brushed the bruise on her face

have a *care, love/good cry out/rest now*

have been chattering on and you will think me a featherhead

having been rusticated because his *grandfather/father/uncle/whoever* refused to pay his gambling debts

he had to own ~ admit

he owes me a favor, so this morning I went round to call in my debt

he paced around the parlor in long, angry strides, his hands curled into fists

he sold out his commission

he'd allow her that ~ give her

he'd ridden hell for leather

he'd thought never to darken England's shores again

he's madder than a hornet

heart stilled in his chest as he watched

heels over head in love ~ head over heels

helped her disembark

helps to be on good terms with the good Ladies Patronesses

her fingers on the harp were light and sure

her flirtatious behavior was truly beyond the pale

her maid had threaded *deep blue/whatever color* ribbon and seed pearls through her hair

her small, even stitches bound the garment together

her strangled cry echoed in his ears as he watched *whoever* crumple to the ground, a hideous scarlet stain marring the perfection of his snowy white dinner jacket

his arm tightening possessively around her

his *brows raising sharply/mind raced*

his grandfather told him he looked 'demmed ridiculous'

his polished Wellingtons clicking softly with his swift stride

his walking stick clicking lightly against the pavement

I am for home

I believe *I feel a bout of the megrims coming on/we will rub along well enough together*

I *must/need be* away

I shall *be back anon/have her back here in a trice*

I wouldn't go in there; the Countess is in high dudgeon ~ bad mood

I'll allow ~ I'll agree

I'll wager it

I'm rejoining my ships

I've business to attend, Parliament to sit, and people with whom to hobnob

icy dread tiptoed down her spine

in an effort to befool society and the queen

in view of half the *ton's* tabbies

is your *brother/father/uncle* to Town this Season

just gone off for a lie-down

kicked him in the shin, but her soft slipper didn't cause so much as a flinch

lamplighters had finished their task

landed a facer ~ punched someone in the face

left in a dudgeon ~ high offense/deep resentment

let us *away/cry* peace

let's have it done. Let's not

let's make our way there, what

levée ~ an early afternoon assembly held by the King or Queen, to which only men were admitted

lifted a hand and tipped his hat in a sign of deference and respect

lifting her skirts, she ran from the room

like anyone else of his class, adhered to the notion

lips pursed with a sour expression

London became a marriage market during the Season. Both men and women looking for a spouse, and all within a few months' time. Girls had to be presented to the Queen before being able to enter society. All titled ladies were eligible to be presented, along with the wives and daughters of these professions: clergy, military and naval officers, physicians and barristers, (considered aristocratic professions,) but not wives or daughters of General Practitioners or solicitors. She had to be presented by a lady of higher rank, whether family member or friend

made a devil of a stir at the time

made *another faux pas/her a stiff, formal bow*

making an utter hash of this

managed to complete her toilette quickly

may I have permission to ascertain if there are any breaks?

May signified the 'official' start of the season with an annual exhibition at the Royal Academy of Art. A whirlwind of court balls, concerts, private balls and dances, parties and sporting events began

men retreated to the smoking parlor for their whiskey and cigars

might I have a word?

might risk catching a catarrh ~ cold

must away to London

must either pay court to her or leave her alone

needed to take a wife to ensure the marquessate

no doubt grinning like a bedlamite

no one seemed interested in seeking out their bed

nodded and strode swiftly down the *marble/carpeted* corridor

offered her his arm and led the procession to the formal dining room

oh, I am in the basket now ~ in trouble

on a typical day in the season, families rose early to ride in Hyde Park. Rotten Row, a sandy track, was *the* place to be seen, or the Ladies' Mile for women. Ladies trained throughout their girlhood to become experts in mounting, riding gracefully while still in command of the horse, shaking hands with friends from the saddle, and dismounting. They also learned to control their horse to avoid accidents in crowded situations

on his feet, crouched with his sword drawn before

on the morning of his leave-taking he

on the verge of making a complete cake of herself

once consent for marriage was reached and the father involved, legal documents would be drawn

once marriage settlements were reached, the bride and her mother busied themselves planning the upcoming festivities

once presented, a prospective bride could reasonably attend 50 balls, 60 parties, 30 dinners and 25 breakfasts all in one season. If she didn't marry within two or three seasons, she was considered a failure, and at 30 a hopeless spinster

or find himself legshackled against his will

Papa would have an apoplexy if he had known

perhaps *if you weren't such a layabed you'd have been/you ought to take a spot of air*

pinched her cheeks to keep them rosy

placing his cane on the floor, he placed both his hands atop the ivory knob that formed the handle

planted her palms firmly in the middle of his chest and pushed

plotting to stick his spoon into the wall ~ kill him

pray *don't try to cozen me just to be polite/enlighten me*

pressed her elegantly gloved fingers to his chest

preyed upon single ladies like a hound on the hunt for foxes promenade ~ area set aside for walking

propped his walking stick against a nearby table

propping his shoulders against the mantelpiece

proved himself to be quite the rake

purchasing a trousseau. It was customary to send a daughter off to her new marriage with new clothing, gloves

pursed her lips with amusement

pushed her back down on the settee lest she faint again

put a thick baize under the tablecloth. This prevents noise and is quite indispensable

quit the chamber

raising some kind of breeze ~ up to mischief

rang a fine peal over ~ yelled at

ready to banish him to perdition ~ hell

refolded the missive and placed it on the stack of mail on the silver tray on his oaken desk

reminded him of a hound on the scent of a fox

rested his head against the high back of the chair

retired to the smoking room to enjoy their cigars

ribbons festooned the kissing ball of holly, ivy, rosemary and mistletoe

riding neck-or-nothing is going to get him seriously injured ~ with complete abandon; recklessness

rode horseback rather than in an equipage

rose and picked up her cloak. “Direct me to the nearest posting-house, please.”

rubbing the drying cloth over his head and body

running neck-or-nothing alongside ~ desperate, with complete abandon and recklessness

ruthlessly pursued and seduced by a rogue

said with a chilling calm

Season ~ coincided with the sitting of Parliament. This began any time after Christmas, depending upon the success of the hunting season in the country. The season usually began in earnest after Easter session break, since many families remained in country until midwinter or even as late as March

seldom ventured far from London

selling his commission

sent them down the steps to their waiting carriages

set her teacup and saucer aside

set his crystal snifter on the small table beside his chair

settled the chair back on all four legs

shall all be put to the blush ~ embarrassed

shall I wish you happy?

she *faltered, seemingly at a loss for words/struggled to draw a calming breath*

she was in the suds for sure ~ in trouble

she'd *done it up brown this time/never be accepted by the* ton

shrugged as if it was of little or no import

slammed his fist into his jaw. The man dropped like a stone

slammed his fist on the roof, a signal to stop the carriage

sliding a brass warming pan between the sheets to chase away the chill

smitten by Cupid's arrow

sniffed haughtily

Sporting Events ~ The Derby was an event for the masses, held in May or June. Parliament adjourned for this race. Ascot was more exclusive, and attended by the upper classes. The season peaked in the June fortnight between Derby and Ascot. July hosted the Henley Regatta and cricket contests, with attention given to school rivals Oxford and Cambridge, and Eton and Harrow

sputtering with frustration

St Bartholomew's Fair was held in August every year from 1133 to 1855 in London in the area known as West Smithfield and was opened by the Lord Mayor of London. Over time the Fair developed a reputation as visitors to the Fair often had too much to drink and sometimes behaved badly—so the slang term,

Bartholomew Baby, came to indicate someone who was drunk and not behaving well

stalked away in a thundering rage

stared out into the gaslit street

stirred on the chaise

stood and snuffed out his cheroot

stopped a handful of paces from

strolled the well-tended garden paths

struck a lucifer on the mantelpiece and held it to the paper ~ match

struggled to keep his surprise hidden

stuck her fork in the wall ~ died

studied a bundle of letters that had arrived with the afternoon post

surveyed herself in the Cheval glass ~ a tall mirror fitted at its middle to an upright frame so that it can be tilted

tapped his crop *impatiently against his thigh/against her gloved palm*

tapped his walking stick on the man's shoulder

tapping off his ash (cheroot)

that started the bloody rucktion ~ a violent and unpleasant row

the blood drained away from her face at the thought of pricking *her uncle's/whoever's* ire

the gloved hand of her dance partner resting lightly on her waist as they twirled

the man shrugged out of his greatcoat, hung it behind the door and strode to the fire. He stretched his large hands to the blaze

the others gathered in the parlor before dinner

the parlor door opened and *whoever* breezed in

the Patronesses have approved her unanimously and have given her a voucher

The Season ~ officially began when Parliament re-opened in London—late January through early July—and was an endless whirl of social events–balls, dances, masquerades, military reviews, theatre parties, and other social pleasures to be enjoyed by the *ton*. Families with marriageable children used the Season to present them to the *ton* in hopes of arranging profitable marriages. Thus, the Season can also be referred to as the 'Marriage Mart.' For girls, the Season was an intense period of social interacting in which any misstep or breach of proper etiquette could spread through gossip circles at Almack's like wildfire and conceivably ruin her marriage and social prospects within the *ton*

the sensation snaked down to her belly and lower

to *collect his rents/prevent the marquisate from*

to get rid of the megrims

to marry her

to set one's cap ~ try to catch a husband

took a seat on the richly upholstered silk sofa

took the liberty of addressing her by her first name, though she had never given him license

turning up the wick on the oil lamp

used a mounting block

waiting to spring the parson's mousetrap

walked out onto the street to hail a passing hansom cab

was hysterical when he learned *whomever* would marry, because he'd always thought she would belong with him

was not happy when he saw her. He turned to the peer who had brought her from *whatever country event*

will stay here and have a nice quiet coze with ~ chat

wish *me happy/you joy of this frippery*

wish someone at Jericho ~ wish them gone

with quick, efficient jerks he stripped off his gloves

wondering what piece of salacious gossip she would be regaled with today

would *have had a fit of vapors had she seen/worry about what London's society would say*

would you like? ~ do you fancy

would you really kill me? In a trice

wound their way through the snarl of horses and carriages

F. Dancing

~

an Allemande began

as they executed the complex steps

at a ball, the hostess provided dressing rooms (retiring rooms) for ladies and gentlemen, with at least one servant in each to handle guests' needs. A complete set of toilet articles was supplied in the dressing rooms for emergencies

balls and dances started at 10:00 p.m. and went until about 3:00 a.m. Musicians played an equal number of waltzes and quadrilles, with one or two other dances. Available programmes listed the schedule of dances. Balls normally opened with a minuet, followed by a quadrille

contrived to dominate her dance card

cotillion ~ French dance for four or more couples

country dance ~ a dance of rural English origin in which partners face each other in two long lines

curtsied to the man she'd been dancing with as the set came to a close

engaged in a spirited quadrille

floated across a polished floor in the arms of some handsome young buck

had gone to the ball during the height of the s*eason*

half of Mayfair seemed to promenade and twirl to the sound of

led her through the minuet

may I have the honor of this dance?

minuet ~ usually the first dance at an *assembly/ball*, slow music, small steps, a slow graceful dance for two people

moved silently through the figures

quadrille ~ square dance with four couples several times, he'd glanced her way, only to have the movements of the quadrilles and reels move them in different directions

strains of a sweeping Viennese waltz drifted through the French doors

the orchestra began playing a minuet, the traditional opening set at any ball

the strains of a sweeping Viennese waltz drifted through the French doors that had been opened to let the winter chill cool the spinning, twirling dancers

turned on one heel and reentered the ballroom

will you favor me with this dance?

would you do me the honor of standing up with me on the next dance

G. Time/Time Frames

~

fortnight ~ two weeks

half ~ thirty minutes past the hour

half *one/past* (like 1:30)

has been donkey's years since ~ a very long time

have waited an additional quarter hour

it's nearly half five

on the morrow

outside, he could hear the watch calling midnight

perhaps *Friday/Saturday* next

Saturday fortnight ~ two weeks from this Saturday

sennight ~ one week

the watch ~ people that walked the streets and called out the time at night

Thursday next

twelvemonth ~ year

H. Clothing

1) Women

~

a cloak hung there for any of the servants to use

a frilled widow's cap

a long dark opera cloak

a walking ensemble of dark blue serge

accepted her gloves from the maid

adjusted the ivory fichu around her neck

after a quick wash, she unlaced her stays, pulled her nightrail over her head and leaped

amidst the swish of her skirts

as she set about unbuttoning her boots

attired in a *forest green/or whatever color* riding habit

bandeau ~ a narrow band of stiffened fabric to hold the hair back

began to pick nervously at the skirts of her day dress

Bell's Court and Fashionable Magazine Addressed Particularly to the Ladies was a British women's magazine published from 1806 to 1837

betsy ~ detachable collar comprised of lace ruffles to be worn with different dresses

black crepe dresses for mourning

blue/white/crème silk gown that fit snugly to her generous curves

bonnet ~ a brimless hat that ties under the woman's chin by a ribbon

busk ~ a long, flat board-like item inserted into the front of a full-corset to aid a woman's posture and separate the breasts

chemise ~ shift (slip)

chemisette ~ short linen or muslin shirt, originally part of a riding costume, worn to fill in a wide-necked bodice for day wear - sometimes with a stand-up collar or ruff

choosing a morning dress of silk

cinched her into her corset

clad in a wisp of nothing

claimed the dress was all the crack ~ very fashionable

clothes hung neatly in the wardrobe

corset ~ garment with stays meant to decrease the size of the waist and lift the breasts

cotton stockings completed the necessary undergarments

could feel the whisper of his clothes against hers

cotton or silk stockings, held up by garters

dabbed at her nose with a handkerchief she'd retrieved from her sleeve

décolletage ~ neckline of a low-cut gown

deep blue jacket with a striped waistcoat in shades of *blue and green/gray and black*

deftly untied the ribbons of her chemise

departed in a flurry of skirts and ladies

describing a gown she had seen in *La Belle Assemblee*, the magazine all ladies of fashion avidly sought

domino ~ a short hooded cloak worn with a mask–usually at masquerades

donned a simple silk shirtwaist

drawing up the high fur collar of her pelisse

dress rustling with her movements

dressed her for the afternoon in an embroidered promenade dress and pelisse of rich

dressed in a fashionable *pink/whatever* color muslin *dress/gown*

dressed in a stylish riding habit, a crop in her hand

dressed in *an unadorned dress/his usual dandyish elegance*

dressed in the *first stare/height* of fashion

dull black bombazine of her mourning dress

elegantly attired in a *dark blue/whatever color* riding jacket

evening dress referred to outfits suitable only at evening events; a type of full dress

fichu ~ piece of lace, muslin, or other thin cloth inserted like a scarf and worn about the neck and cleavage to preserve a lady's modesty

fingering the dresses

fingers worked with deft precision to loosen her laces

freed her from her stays

frock ~ (or *smock-frock*) outer garment formerly common in rural Europe

full dress was the most formal dress the women had. It was worn for the most formal occasions, i.e. evening concerts and card parties, soirees, balls, and court occasions

fumbled nervously with her robes

gathered up her fan and reticule

gathering her wide skirts in her hands, she dashed across the front yard

half-boots ~ ankle boots for ladies, could be of kid leather for outdoor wear or of cloth for indoors. Fancy varieties of velvet or silk and decorated with beads or embroidery for wearing with formal clothes could also be found

half dress is considered any dress halfway between undress and full dress, i.e. dressy casual

haute couture ~ high fashion

held the torn pieces of her bodice together and

helped her remove her pelisse

her arms encased in full-length white gloves

her *chemise and drawers/sleep-crumpled chemise*

her cloak provided scant protection

her *curvaceous figure encased in silk and lace/curves soft and natural without the corset*

her gloved hands demurely folded

her heart plunging to her half-boots

her *satin skirts/skirts swished about her ankles as*

her *slippered feet/soft-soled slippers made no sound on*

her *whatever color* morning gown

her *whatever color or patterned* promenade dress made of the lightest muslin

her wretched tight stays

high-waisted low-cut empire dresses (muslin, gauze, crepe, silk, sarsenet, satin)

hiked her skirt and *hurried off/rushed across the*

his hand searched the front of her drawers, found the ribbon edged slit of the garment, and

hurried to the door with a rustle of her full skirts

in a swirl of *pale blue/ivory* muslin

in a swish of skirts

in her satin and velvet cloak

in pastel colors, with short puffed sleeves and short jackets, corsets which lifted up their

it hugged her body (clothes)

ivory sprigged muslin

jumper ~ pullover/sweater

kicked off her slippers and drew on her high-lows ~ lace-up boot with a low heel, reaching to the ankle

kid slippers made little sound

knickers ~ girl's and ladies' underwear

La Belle Assemblée ~ fashion magazine dedicated to the elite of society. Each month it told Englishwomen what was in fashion in London. Now best known for its fashion plates of Regency era styles

lace and beribboned parasol

laced her into her corset

ladies had morning dresses, afternoon dresses and evening dresses

layers of silk organza trailed behind as she moved toward the front of the church

leaned back in her chair and longed to loosen her corset lacings

lifted one elegant shoulder beneath the silk of her gown

light green merino pelisse

long-sleeved premise ~ top

loosened *her bindings/the tapes of her petticoats*

made quick work of her ablutions and donned the blue muslin dress that had been laid out for her

muff ~ round fur-lined accessory for keeping ladies' hands warm

muffler ~ a scarf

muslin ~ fine, thin, semi-transparent cotton available in different finishes. Muslin was the most popular material for ladies' gowns for both day and evening wear

nervous, her finger twisted the ribbon on her bonnet, crushing it beyond repair

no low-necked dresses nor short sleeves should be seen at day receptions, nor white ties or dress coats. Elegant jewelry and laces were also reserved for evening

off-the-peg ~ clothes off the rack rather than hand made

once cinched, hooked, and buttoned she

outfitting their daughters for the visits, dinner parties, and balls that would win them a husband

pattens ~ rings strapped onto the bottom of a woman's shoes or boots to elevate her a few inches above the mud or slush during inclement weather

pelisse ~ a long sleeved 3/4 length lady's jacket; an overdress or coat dress. The pelisse fit close to the figure, although not tight, and had high-waisted lines like some of the dresses. Pelisses were heavily trimmed with such things as fur, swansdown, contrasting fabric, and frog fastenings. For the most part they replaced fur-lined cloaks of earlier periods

picked up her skirts and climbed the stairs

picked/picking up her skirts and *fled/darting back toward*

producing *whatever article* from the hidden pocket in her skirt

pulled on her stockings, combination, camisole and petticoats

pulled up her bodice and tied the knot at her neck

reached for the laces on the front of her gown

redingote ~ long, fitted outdoor coat, belted and open to reveal the skirt of the dress beneath–often trimmed with fur

refastened the top buttons of her pelisse

remove her kidskin gloves

removed her mobcap, and her long dark hair spilled down over her shoulders

reticule ~ small women's handbag, usually made of silk or satin, that draws together at the top with a cord

retrieved a folded white handkerchief from an inner breast pocket and handed it to her

retrieved her reticule from atop the bureau and

ribbons laced through the eyelet edging

riding habit ~ drawers, skirt, basque, and high boots

satin trimmed with white lace and ribbons

she wrestled the wind for control of her hooded traveling cloak

silk day dress

smoothing her *dove-gray/navy blue/whatever color* walking skirt

soft *green/whatever* color day dress and feather-bedecked hat

spencer ~ a short, waist-length jacket, with or without sleeves (tight sleeves when it had them). Generally an outdoor garment worn in the morning or the afternoon, but could also be part of an evening ensemble; similar to a gentleman's riding coat, but without tails

stared at her satiny kid slippers

stays ~ a corset

still in the process of tying her bedrobe

stood in her chemise and stockings

that gown should suit

the beribboned garment

the boning of her corset *dug into her waist/jabbing her painfully in the ribs*

tied her bonnet strings

tights ~ nylons, usually sheer, which also cover the groin, i.e. pantyhose tippet ~ an abbreviated cape similar to a stole or boa; a fancy scarf usually of swansdown or fur

tried to pretend an interest in lace or kid gloves, satin or leather slippers

tucked her handkerchief back in her sleeve

tugged on long *white/ivory/yellow* kid gloves

turned her around and began to unfasten the long row of tiny buttons that ran down the back of her gown

turning back to the armoire, she chose a simple shirtwaist and skirt to wear

undress simply meant casual, informal dress, i.e. the type of dress worn from early morning until noon or perhaps until four or five, depending on one's engagements for the day. Undress was usually more comfortable, more warm, more casual, and much cheaper in cost than half dress or full dress

unmentionables

unpacked her clothes and hung them in the armoire

untied the tapes at her waist. Her drawers dropped to the floor

voluminous folds of her skirt

wearing a short, fitted riding jacket of *dark blue/whatever color* with satin cords and brass buttons. Lace peeked from under the cuffs and she could feel the ruffle around her throat. Her long, wool skirt was divided and nearly covered her leather half-boots

whatever color muslin gown and matching bonnet

whatever color silk gown that fit snugly to her generous curves

whatever color skirt over layered petticoats ruffling softly

whirled off in a flurry of pastels and lace

white/whatever color muslin gown with *blue/whatever color* spencer jacket and matching hat

with chemises underneath

wore a *whatever color* pelisse and matching bonnet

worked the buttons on her gown

wrung her hands in the silken folds of her day dress

2) Men

~

a flowing, flawless cravat

a pair of tight fawn-colored pantaloons, gleaming white waistcoat, and hunter green riding jacket

a patterned waistcoat

adding the stockings, breeches, waistcoat, jacket, watch fob, gloves and shoes

although he was handsome in his black coat and breeches, she could imagine how magnificent his

an ivory silk waistcoat

as always, he was in prime twig ~ well-dressed man; fashionably dressed

banyan ~ men's dressing gown

beaver hat ~ black top hat made of beaver skin, waterproof

began to unbutton his silk waistcoat

black tailcoat and snowy white cravat

bracers ~ over-the-shoulder straps to support slacks, i.e. suspenders

braces ~ suspenders

breeches ~ short close-fitting men's trousers that fastened just below the knees and were worn with stockings

breeches that *clung/molded* to his muscular thighs

buckskins ~ fashionable trousers made from deerskin

buff breeches with browns and greens, more like a country gentleman

buff colored breeches

buff pantaloons tucked into gleaming Hessians

clad in black tails, white silk waistcoat and expertly tied neckcloth

clapping his top hat on his head

cravat ~ gentleman's neckcloth, usually made of silk, starching and tying must be precise; crucial to the wearer's fashionable appearance. Part of a valet's job was to know the fine art of cravat tying. White for formal occasions; informal could be black, any other color, or patterned

cut a dashing figure in his smoking jacket

doffed his hat *and cloak and handed them to the maid/in a sweeping elegant gesture*

dressed for this evening's affair in long coat and tailored breeches

dressed to go out, his cape draped over his shoulders

dressed with flawless elegance

drew off his gloves

epaulet ~ ornamental shoulder pad on military uniforms

expertly wound and tied his cravat in the fashionable mathematical style

facings ~ material of a different color that showed when cuffs or collar were folded over—in the military, different colored facings implied different regiments

false calves ~ padding for a man's calves to fill out his stockings to have a more muscular look–worn with knee breeches

fingered the edge of his hat nervously

flicked an imaginary fleck of lint from his sleeve of black superfine cloth

fob pocket ~ a small pocket at the front waistline of a man's trousers to hold a watch

formal dark *whatever color* suit, black waistcoat, and silk neck cloth

fussed over the tying of his cravat

gave him a weary smile and loosened his cravat

gleaming Hessians

got to his feet and straightened his waistcoat

grabbed his threadbare coat and stormed out

grasped his watch chain and removed the pocket watch from his vest

greatcoat ~ an outdoor overcoat for men usually with at least one, often several capes, around the shoulders

grey pin stripe/whatever color three piece suit

hat pulled low on his forehead

he *cut a fine form indeed/doffed his hat*

he paused to unbutton the fall of his trousers and free himself

he was in prime twig ~ a well-dressed man or woman is said to be in prime twig

Hessian boots ~ men's mid-calf boots coming to just below the knee or lower that have tassels on the top

high collar-points shooting up over their flawless tired cravats

high-crowned beaver hat

his black frockcoat looked like it had been molded to his broad shoulders

his cravat *disordered/impeccably tied in the mathematical*

his *diamond/emerald/whatever gem* stickpin glinting in the folds of his snowy white cravat

his high starched collar-points grazed his chin

his *highly polished beaver hat/shiny boots glittered in the sunlight*

his perfectly pressed suit and polished shoes bespoke a man of means

his shoulders *rippled beneath the fine clothes/strained the material of his shirt*

his thighs strained against the cloth of his *black/whatever color* trousers

his top boots had been polished to a high gleam

his valet eyed him with disdain. The single-breasted jacket had 4 buttons and a small notched lapel and two flap pockets on either side as well as a ticket pocket on the right. A white pocket square, in his chest pocket, was made of cotton or linen. The sleeves had 3 cuff buttons and the shoulder seam was located further back than on most coats of the day

his white day shirt had a detachable collar with little wings, and around the neck he had a *whatever color* tie with a discrete *whatever color* tie stick pin. The sleeves and sleevehead showed distinct wrinkles

his wrinkled *cravat/linen shirt* lent a disheveled air to

homburg ~ a formal felt hat characterized by a dent running down the center of the crown (a 'gutter crown'), a stiff brim shaped in a 'kettle curl'

impossibly complicated folds of his snowy neckcloth

in his waistcoat pocket he carried a fob watch held in place by a decorative chain

inexpressibles ~ *breeches/men's pants*, although none would actually say the word 'pants'

jacket emphasized the width of his shoulders

kerseymere ~ light-weight fabric perfect for breeches, a type of wool

knee breeches ~ knee length trousers worn with stockings; fit snugly

lawn shirts and silk cravats

linen ~ inexpensive strong light-weight cloth, used primarily for men's shirts and undergarments - comes in several weaves, including lawn and cambric

livery ~ male servant's uniform including frock coat, knee breeches, white stockings, and pumps (shoes), along with a powdered wig. Grooms attending carriages also wore livery, topped it off with a tricorne hat

long sleeves with vandyked cuffs

looking perfectly bored as he neatened the cuffs of his shirt

looking resplendent in his flowing black evening cloak

men always wear black to Almacks

men can wear whatever color hankie they want–as long as it's white ☺

men don't wear trousers to Almacks

muscles rippling beneath his fine linen shirt

nankeen ~ lightweight yellowish cotton cloth popular for men's pantaloons

nearly colliding with a man in coattails and top hat

neckcloth embellished with a glittering *diamond/emerald/ whatever gem* stickpin

oilcloth coat ~ raincoat

pantaloons ~ men's pants that gained popularity, eventually lengthening into the full length trouser

pants ~ underpants of poor quality. Although refers to trousers in parts of Northern England

physique looked muscled and lean in dress uniform

producing a crisp handkerchief from his coat pocket

pumps ~ low-heeled, unadorned black or brown shoe worn by men; formal footwear as an alternative to boots. Could sometimes have an understated bow or tassel

pushing his frock coat off and to the floor

removed his *overcoat and hat and gave them to the footman/top hat*

removing his elegant greatcoat

rich black evening attire

shrugged his shoulders in his frock coat

shrugged off his evening coat and tore at the knot of his cravat until it fell free

smalls ~ underclothing, underwear, particularly underpants

smoking jacket of quilted satin and velvet

straightened his cravat and patted down the front of his pristine white shirt, tugging at the sleeves of his dinner jacket

straightened the French cuffs on his silk shirt

suspenders ~ elasticized support for stockings

tall silk hat

the wind billowed his *black/dark* greatcoat

throwing down his greatcoat and gloves on the back of a chair

tugged at his shirt collar and longed to unfasten the top button

tugged his waistcoat back in place

tugged on his starched shirt points to make them stand in place against his raw cheeks

tugging at his cravat as if to neaten it

twirling his greatcoat down from his shoulders with a flourish unbuttoned his waistcoat

unfastened his trousers and kicked off his boots

unpacking *Lord whoever's* portmanteaux into the polished mahogany wardrobe

vest ~ garment, usually sleeveless, worn under a shirt, i.e. undershirt

was dressed in a fashionable fawn-coloured cutaway jacket and the new odd-looking trousers

wearing a great coat and top hat

wearing a heavy, single breasted, over knee-length overcoat in grayish blue

well-polished black knee high boots

Wellingtons ~ boots

whatever color pantaloons hugged long, muscular thighs

white ruffled shirts, high stiff collars, dark long tailcoats (cut short in front), white cravat, knee breeches, stockings, black buckled pumps. In the daytime, men frequently wore tall hats and Hessian boots

white shirtsleeves rolled against his forearms

with his long, black greatcoat swirling about his boots

withdrew a pistol from its carriage holder and dropped it into a pocket inside his greatcoat

wore a *long, black frock coat/mourning band on his arm*

I. Bow/Curtsy

~

bobbed a curtsy

bowed *gallantly/his acknowledgement*

bowed stiffly and handed up the reins

bowed with ready grace

curtseyed deeply to his bow

dipped *into/them both* a curtsy

extended her hand to him as she sank into a perfect curtsy

gave a firm bob of the head

he said, taking up her hand and bowing over it

sketched a *bow/curtsy*

swept off his hat and made a quick bow

J. Glasses/Quizzing Glass/Lorgnette/Monocle

he removed his wire-rimmed spectacles and began to polish them with a handkerchief

just finished a book today where the hero sported a monocle

lifted his quizzing glass and squinted through the eyepiece

looking through his quizzing glass

producing his quizzing glass with a flourish

removing his pince-nez, he polished them

took up her lorgnette and peered through the lens

K. Timepiece/Watch

fob ~ short chain or ribbon with an attached medallion or ornament connected to a man's pocketwatch

glanced at his timcpiece

reached inside his coat, fingering the case of his pocket watch

returning his timepiece to his pocket, he

snapped the timepiece shut

L. Servants

a coterie of liveried coachmen spilled out

a downstairs maid in a gray serge gown with a snowy white apron and a stiffly starched white cap

a footman *hastened to open the door/stood rigidly at atten*tion

a house maid quickly laid the fire and tidied the grate

about to find himself dismissed without a character (reference)

above stairs

admitted him to the salon, announcing him to

allowed the maid to dress her hair

as the servants cleared the soiled dishes

batman ~ orderly assigned to a military officer

been working as a tweeny

below stairs

bobbed a slap-dash curtsy, then

brushing the shoulders of the master's coat

butler ~ responsible for the activities of the entire male household staff; he was in charge of the wine cellar and the household's silver and china; answered doors and dealt with visitors, so had to be aware of social distinctions and proper etiquette. Unlike lower servants, the butler was always called by his surname

butler maintained his position directly behind the *viscount/earl/duke/etc.*—or for those that employed a steward, the butler would report to the steward

butlers and housekeepers kept a strict eye on their staff and required employees to mind the proprieties

chamber maids (or housemaids) were responsible for carrying coal, lighting fires, heating water for washing and bathing and carrying it upstairs to the bedrooms. They also cleaned chamber pots, changed bed linens, drew the curtains, and scrubbed the floors

charwoman ~ woman hired to clean a place

coachmen cared for and drove the coaches

companion or governess ~ station above the household's hired servants, but below the family

cook (male chef in a great house) traditionally employed by the master or mistress of the house. They often received a salary higher even than the steward and as such were regarded as separate from the rest of the domestic staff

country estates often employed a gamekeeper to breed and feed game courtship frowned upon with the staff

crossed to the bed and folded back the counterpane

dairymaids or milkmaids milked cows and churned butter on country estates that had special servants for such tasks

disappeared into the shadows of the servants' wing

dismissing the footman with a terse nod

dour-looking servants

dropped a wordless curtsy

dustman ~ man who came around to collect the refuse from fires burned for cooking and warmth

each butler would have a measuring stick for setting the table; everything must be in a precise setting

female staff had to leave service if they became pregnant

first footman always takes in the meat

footman ~ male servant under the authority of the butler. They served at meals, accompanied ladies of the house on errands and social calls, and looked after the lamps and candles in a house. Since their duties included elements of a bodyguard or bouncer, footmen tended to be tall and imposing. Many wore old-fashioned livery with knee-breeches and powdered wigs as part of their uniform

footmen closing the double doors on the stroke of eleven, barring entry to any unfortunate who was late ~ Almack's

gardener often had assistants beneath him for tending homes that had extensive grounds

gave her housekeeper a gentle squeeze

gentlemen of great wealth and importance more often than not employed a steward—a personal assistant—whose duties included management of the domestic staff. Beneath the steward, or at the top of the hierarchy for large households that did not employ a steward, came the butler and housekeeper

governess ~ woman hired to *teach/care for* the families' children, ranked higher than the remainder of the house servants

gravel outside raked first thing every morning by footman

groom ~ servant who cared for the horses, assisted by stableboys

handed his cape to the footman

he's very loyal to the family ~ servant

helped the maids and footmen clear away the last of the glassware and littered dance cards and valentines

her black skirts rustling as she poured the tea

her little maiden room she shared with *another maid/servant*, with its neatly made single beds and

her voice was quiet, deferential, as befitted her new position as an employee of the *whatever* family

his valet lathered his chin for shaving

housekeeper ~ top ranking female servant responsible for everything in a house with the exception of cooking and kitchen duties, which are under the duties of the Cook. The housekeeper's responsibilities include cleaning, laundry, household maintenance, and supervising all the maids. She maintained the household accounts, managed the linens, prepared coffee, tea, and preserves. Wore a chatelaine around her waist or neck – keys to every room in the house. Even if she was unmarried, everyone called her 'Mrs.' as a sign of respect

housekeeper, butler, and cook were the main servants in the household

I'll send someone in to lay a fire straightaway

ill prepared for the onslaught of servants and mayhem

kitchenmaid ~ kitchen servants who lit the stoves and helped Cook prepare meals; ranked above scullerymaid

lady's maid ~ woman who cared for the mistress'—or other female relatives'—clothes, dressing, grooming, and mending; considered an upstairs servant answerable only to her mistress, not the housekeeper. A lady's maid styled hair, helped her mistress dress and undress and maintained her wardrobe. She might also read aloud or massage her mistress's temples when she had a headache

lining up the staff by rank to greet *whoever*

looked every inch the professional whip ~ coachman

maid ~ her plain black pelisse and unadorned felt bonnet

maids-in-waiting

manservant

marched smartly toward the servant stairs

men and women staff had separate sleeping quarters

no more faithful servant than I

nursemaids were usually under age twenty and were the only female servants who spent much time out of the house, as they took the small children they cared for, for daily walks

opened the baize door with her back and twirled deftly through

prominence of the person served proved far more important than the servant's length of service to the family

pulling the silken cord that hung by the door, servants quickly laid in a fire

ran a finger over the sideboard checking for dust

rankings even extended to the servants of those visiting the household

rushing about giving last minute instructions to the servants

scullery maids and laundry maids did the most difficult and painful work; lowest in the servant hierarchy

scullery maids used cleansing agents such as harsh abrasives like sand and lye. With lavish multi-course dinner parties all the fashion, scullery maids often worked long hours cleaning the hundreds of dirty dishes generated during such affairs

servant came quickly from the shadows

servants quickly laid in a fire

servants stationed several paces behind their chairs

servants were preparing the evening meal

skivvy ~ scullery maid or lowest servant doing menial work; somebody at the bottom of the pecking order

snatched up her ladyship's tray

spent far too many years in servitude

steward worked closely with the master of the house, and often in the master's absence, performed day to day tasks in his stead; butler would defer to him

the butler arrived with *his/person's name* hat in his hand, then turned to open the door

the butler secured the door againt the wind

the butler's respectful voice pulled him from his thoughts

the footman at the rear of the carriage hastened round to lower the steps

the footman placed a moveable step beneath the carriage and assisted her as she emerged

the invisible, but ever-present, servants

the quiet burden of their service

the rattle of a servant cleaning a grate bestirred him sometime near dawn

the scullery maid banked the kitchen fire for the night

the valet stood back to admire his handiwork

those who wished to portray themselves as having an air of middle-class respectability employed domestic help

thrilled by her elevation to the status of lady's maid

tongue-lashing a scullery maid

tossed his hat to a footman and handed his gloves to the butler

tumbling one of the kitchen maids

turnover within most household positions averaged about every two to three years—often even more frequently than that for the lower positions

tweeny ~ a maid who assists both cook and housemaid

upper housemaids performed duties requiring direct interaction with the family and visitors, so, like footmen, they were often expected to be more presentable in appearance and manners than the lower housemaids who were responsible for heavier and dirtier work

upper house maids often in charge of decorating

upper servants dined apart from, and before, the lower servants

valet, aka 'gentleman's gentleman', acted as the gentleman of the house's personal barber, assisted him to dress and undress, and maintained his wardrobe. Valet rhymes with 'ballot'

very good, sir

very good, your ladyship ~ yes

walked out on her half-day with the footman

was an excellent coachman

waved *away the servants and waited for them to depart before speaking/the servant away*

went belowstairs with a great sense of trepidation

with a curt nod *for/to* the footman, he swept into

with a diplomatic bow her butler smoothly withdrew

without a character to recommend you ~ references

you forget your station

your humble servant, Miss *whoever*

your servant, *lady/My Lord whoever*

M. Conveyances

*~

"Walk on," he commanded, and the vehicle lurched forward

a black barouche/climbed into the travelling carriage

a carriage slowed in the street

a finely appointed footman, dressed in *whatever color* livery, tipped his hat to her and swept the carriage door open

a footman accompanied him to a carriage waiting outside

a footman put down the steps and opened the carriage door

after the carriage rolled to a stop, she took the footman's proffered hand

all the gifts for my family were in the boot of the post-chaise

barouche ~ a fancy horse drawn carriage with four wheels and pulled by two horses, having a C-spring suspension system, and a soft cover overhead for those inside

buggy ~ 2-wheeled horse-drawn lightweight carriage

cabriolet ~ light, two-wheeled carriage, one horse. Seated two and was usually driven by the gentleman himself, had a folding leather hood and a perch in the back for the 'tiger' or groom

chaise ~ horse drawn carriage with two wheels, driven by a servant, top could be put down on nice days - similar to our convertibles, can carry four people

coach ~ a carriage that could carry six people, driven by a driver sitting high in front of them

coach pulled a stop in front of the inn

demanding his carriage be brought

dispatched the departing carriages into the night's thick fog

dogcart a sturdy, two-wheeled carriage used by sportsmen because it had a special compartment in the back for hunting dogs

driving his new sporting vehicle down

equipage ~ carriage and all the livery necessary to outfit it

fell back against the leather upholstery as the carriage merged into traffic

footman put down a step for her and help up a gloved hand

gave orders for a carriage to be brought round for them

gazed out the post chaise window

get the baruche

gig ~ lightweight one-horse carriage, held two people, one of them being the driver–used mainly in the country

go and fetch *whomever* with the carriage

hackney coach ~ Regency version of a taxi cab, drawn by four horses, often an old, beat-up carriage of the nobility

his carriage waited beneath the porte-cochère

jarvey ~ slang for a hackney coach driver

landau ~ a four-wheeled fancy horse drawn carriage, similar to a coach, with a two piece hood that can either be left up, or opened. Has double seats facing each other, seating four passengers, with a place in front for the coachman. Two to four horses

mail coach ~ coaches with regular routes and schedules that carried both mail and passengers around the country

packet ~ ship running regular, short-distance routes, carrying mail and passengers

preceded them out of the carriage and handed them down

relaxed back into the plush leather upholstery of the carriage

sent a carriage for her

the badly sprung carriage pitched

the carriage *bounced and his head cracked against the roof/drew up beside them*

the carriage jerked into motion, tossing her against the carriage's leather squab

the carriage rocked *and swayed/to a halt*

the light curricle bounced and jostled *along/over* the uneven road

the rich velvet of the softly upholstered squabs

tilburies ~ light, two-wheeled, open carriage with a bench seat, used in the 1800s

urged the horses forward with an impatient flick of the ribbons (curricle)

when her skirts brushed against his trousers as she settled back on the carriage squab earlier he'd subtly shifted away, as though he found even the merest accidental touch distasteful

without waiting for the footman he opened the door himself

yellow bounder ~ a hired post chaise. Its body was yellow

N. Foodstuffs

*~

after dinner was finished, the tablecloth was removed and wine decanters were set on the table. Women could stay and have some wine before departing for the Drawing Room; men often stayed there drinking for hours–unless they were going out

afternoon tea

apple coffyns ~ apple pastry

balanced a bit of fruit compote on his spoon before he looked up

bangers and mash ~ sausage and mashed potatoes

biscuit ~ baked sweet or savoury cake-like item, usually flat, which is hard when baked and softens over time

braised duckling

bread types ~ pandemain—deemed the best as the flour—was sifted 2 or 3 times; wastel–a good quality bread; cocket–a cheaper, white bread; cheat–wholewheat with the bran removed; tourte–containing husk as well as flour (known as brown bread); horse bread–beans, peas and any general grain was used; clapbread–barley bread or oatcakes. Pandemain was made from wheat and mainly enjoyed by the rich while the usual fare of the common man was a choice of tourte, horse bread or clapbread. Wealthy people often used brown bread as plates (trenchers). Large loaves would be cut into very thick slices and a hollow made in the center. Used trenchers would often be collected and given to the poor to eat

breakfast traditionally eaten around 10:00 a.m. – lasted about an hour

bubble and squeak ~ dish of cooked cabbage fried with cooked potatoes and other vegetables. Often made from the remains of the Sunday roast trimmings

candied fruits

cheese and biscuits after the meals

cherry coffyn ~ danish

chocolate ~ refers to the drink, hot chocolate

clotted cream

copper pans replaced clay pots for cooking

course after course of delectable fare

crisps ~ potato chips

cuppa ~ tea

delicate iced cakes

dinner ~ first course traditionally soup; second course would be when roasted meat would be served, sweet and savoury pies and tarts would be started, and also the game and fish courses; vegetables served in a butter sauce would now be served. Dessert would soon follow.

dinner is served, your ladyship

dinner was usually served at 6 p.m. (countryside) or up until 8 p.m. (town), followed by a soiree or opera

during Georgian times, a single cake—or pudding—could use one dozen eggs and several pints of cream

eel pie

elegant teas and soirees

enjoy tea and scones

entrée ~ starter of a meal (traditionally, the course served between the fish and the joint)

Fat Rascals ~ soft currant biscuits

fetch a glass on the sideboard

foods usually available for breakfast were coffee, hot chocolate, tea, plum cake, pound cake, hot rolls, cold rolls, bread and butter and toast

fortified wines ~ port, Madeira, Marsala, and sherry are considered fortified wines as they are mixed with Brandy or another heavy liquor. This was originally done to preserve the wines while being shipped long distances; also lent a sweetness to the wine

freshened her cup of tea

fruit laden epergnes

full English breakfasts contained eggs, tomatoes, beans, bacon (somewhat like Canadian bacon)

Georgian cooking was very rich—lots of butter, cream and eggs

glass of warm milk sprinkled with nutmeg, a sure cure for the megrims

goblets of wine

hamper ~ large basket for food

helped herself to still-warm coddled eggs and ham from the chafing dish and carried it to the table

ice houses came into being during the Georgian period

in upper and middle class households, food was prepared by multiple staff

introduction of the pudding cloth for boiled puddings made boiling foods more prevalent

jacket potato ~ baked potato

jam making using fruit became popular

jelly ~ a fruit flavoured dessert set with gelatin

join me for tea in the sitting room after you have had time to refresh yourselves

just a drop of tea please ~ several fluid ounces

kippers for breakfast

light breakfasts would have been cakes, i.e. honey cake, plum cake, pound cake, etc.

loaves of cocket bread

Madeira ~ sweet white dessert wine

meals for poorer people were traditionally cooked in one pot, with a muslin bag separating the vegetables

mince ~ ground beef

most kitchen utensils were of copper or wood

most meals still cooked on open fires or spits

muffin ~ a thick round baked yeast roll, usually toasted and served with butter, i.e. English muffin

negus ~ often served shortly before guests left for the evening – made from calves foot jelly, wine, boiling water, lemon and spices

never in her life had she eaten a meal with so many courses

nuncheon ~ new during the Regency period; served between 1-3– were small triangular shaped sandwiches eaten using a knife and fork. Usually only women ate this since most men weren't home at this time of day

pasty ~ hard pastry shell filled with meat and vegetables

peppermint tea for upset stomachs

perhaps we can have *a cup of tea*. Perhaps not

placed the second course of glazed pheasant and apple compote in front of her

placed the service on the sideboard (tea)

Plum Pudding

poorer people ate on wooden plates or thin tinware

potatoes had been regarded as poisonous until the end of the 17th century when they started appearing in meals

poured herself a steaming cup of tea

pressing apple cider

pudding ~ dessert course of a meal

rashers ~ cuts of bacon

refilled their coffee cups from the silver server

Regency period Teas ~ Earl Grey/Ceylon/Russian

ringing in each course with timed precision ~ butler

savored a perfectly prepared lobster bisque

savoury tarts

scones *and custard cakes/with marmalade*

serviette ~ napkin

serving the roast beef, potato soufflé, and salmon in aspic

set aside her teacup and napkin

shared a silver platter

slathered fresh-churned butter onto yeast rolls

smoked salmon roulades

soft currant biscuits

spices became easily obtainable from around the world and were liberally used during the Georgian period

staying for a glass of gooseberry wine and a slice of seed cake

succulent scent of roasted fowl

supper (aka the tea board) usually served around 10:00-11:00 p.m. – a light meal such as soup

sweet ~ an after-meal dessert, i.e. *candy*

tea ~ afternoon snack, i.e. late *lunch;* evening meal (sometimes called *high tea*)

tea and crumpets

tea and hot chocolate were the preferred morning drinks

teapot hidden in a quilted cozy

the courses arrived: 1) beginning with the soup and fish dishes (consommé, poached salmon); 2) meat dishes; 3) sweets course–jellies, blancmange, small iced cakes

the savory aroma of mutton assaulted his senses

the taste of this morning's coddled eggs climbed up the back of her throat

the tea cup clinking softly

the wealthy ate on silver and pewter, and toward the end of the 18th century on china

their cooks had labored long over

tomatoes didn't become popular until the end of the Georgian period

took a plate, serving *himself/herself* from the warming dishes and salvers on the buffet

toward the end of the Regency period ranges came into being; they had a cast iron oven on one side and a water heater on the other

treacle ~ molasses

went to the sideboard and piled his plate high with food

with a generous helping of clotted cream

O. Manners

*~

each butler would have a measuring stick for setting the table

evening gloves must lay in your lap while you are at dinner

mindless of etiquette he

people must sit up straight, no slouching

sitting up straight; never lean back against a chair in the dining room

table laid precisely with silver and linen

unable to forgo all the manners bred into her from infancy, she

wiped the corner of her mouth with her cloth napkin

P. Drinking

*~

a cup of brandy laced milk to soothe her nerves
already well into his cups and the night was still young
bosky ~ drunk
brandy-laced breath
deep in his cups
downed a dram of brandy
downed another mouthful of *coffee/mead/whiskey*
downed the contents
downed their portions in a single swallow
elbow-crooker ~ person who drinks too much
foxed ~ inebriated
had been foxed at the time
half-sprung
he placed the brandy snifter on a round table
I'm a bourbon man myself, but
in his drunken befuddled state
left the lot of them deep in their cups
legless ~ extremely drunk
may I offer you a glass of Madeira?
on the cut ~ drinking binge
pub ~ public house/bar
putting his glass on the table in the dimly lit parlour
stalked to the cellaret to pour himself a brandy
swallowing a healthy dose of his drink
swirled the expensive cognac in his snifter
the smell of the claret on his breath
took a dainty sip of brandy
wasn't drunk, just lightly in his cups
yanked the crystal stopper from a decanter of brandy

Q. Swearing

*~

blister it
bloody hell
but it's damnable
by St. George's sword
claptrap ~ nonsense
claptrap and balderdash
confound it!
damn and blast
damn me if
dash it all
dash it, he
deuce *it/take it*
deuced ~ darned
devil *seize/take* it
fiend seize it ~ damn it
frankly I don't give a whit if
God rot him
good God, leave off
gor blimey ~ exclamation of surprise
he'd be dashed lucky if
heaven forfend ~ heaven forbid
hell's bells
I dashed well don't care
I'm dashed grateful for
I'm deuced if I know
no one gives a jot about
not give a tinker's damn ~ not care
odds fish ~ swearing
on an oath, he

pox rot you

rot *and bother/it*

that's a damned hum ~ lie/false rumour

the devil, you say

the very devil of a day

uttered a string of colorful curses

where in creation was she?

zounds ~ mild oath

R. Monies

*~

annuity ~ a yearly salary that continues as long as the person is alive, i.e. husband to wife

blunt ~ money

cleaned out ~ no money

copper ~ low value coin, copper in color

counted the coins in her hand before putting them in her reticule

financial crisis hit like a sledgehammer

flipped the boy a coin

flush in the pockets ~ rich

ha'penny ~ half a penny

haven't a sixpence to scratch with ~ no money

his pockets are heavy enough

I find myself on the rocks ~ broke, have no money

left her without a sou

never a feather to fly with ~ no money

penny ~ pl. *pence*, or, when referring to coins, *pennies*

pockets to let ~ have no money

purse ~ feminine money container or wallet

purse-pinched ~ have little money

quid ~ pound sterling, i.e. dollar

rolled-up ~ have no money

shilling ~ 12 pennies

swimming in lard ~ very rich

their purses heavy with silver

trying to break someone's shins ~ borrow money

tuppence ~ two pence

wanna put your money on that?

you shall have enough blunt to satisfy even the

S. Games

~

a game of cards might be the very thing to keep her awake and clear her mind of its wayward thoughts

busily collecting his winnings from their completed game of faro

can play at ten penny nails

commerce/whiskey poker ~ card game, players swapped cards that were face up in order to improve their own hands

cribbage ~ card game, players use a cribbage board and pegs to score

customary gathering for charades and whist

draughts ~ checkers

elbow shaker ~ gamester casting dice

faro ~ game of chance favored by gamblers; played at a special table with painted depictions of playing cards around the edges of the table. Men set their chips on the picture of the card they thought the dealer would turn over next

fulhams ~ loaded dice

game of bagatelle ~ billiards derived game

gaming-hell ~ gambling hall

hoodman blind ~ blindman's bluff –1565 ~ a group game in which a blindfolded player tries to catch and identify another player

I think the young people are playing *paille-maille* on the green ~ a lawn game mostly played in the 16th and 17th centuries'–precursor to croquet

patience ~ any of a family of one-player card games, i.e. *solitaire*

played a game of draughts

Pope Joan ~ a popular Victorian family game, an 18th-century English round game of cards for three to eight players

solitaire ~ peg-jumping puzzle game

whist ~ card game

T. Places

~

a hush about Westminster Abbey

a two-story structure that served as a public house and coaching inn

Almack's ~ assembly rooms on Kings Street; balls were held each Wednesday night of the Season; a person had to have a voucher (ticket) to enter and must be personally known by one of the seven patronesses; only the elite of society (*ton*) could attend

Ascot ~ prestigious race horse track, founded by Queen Anne, 1711

assembly room ~ public halls where people gather for dances, concerts, various games/cards, to talk, i.e. Almack's

Astley's Royal Amphitheatre ~ a circus in London featuring horseback riding, acrobats, clowns, etc.

Bath ~ built completely from cream-colored limestone; mosaic tiles depicting mythological gods; glows with warmth and elegance

Bedlam ~ insane asylum in London

Bond Street ~ fashionable shopping street in the West End of London, located in the Mayfair District

Bond Street swarmed with people

Brighton ~ Seaside town about forty-five miles away from London, where people went to improve their health in the craze for sea-bathing—and to party. It was the Prince Regent's favorite vacation resort

Brighton was annually the next stop on the social whirl for high society following the Season in London

Cheapside ~ along with Covent Gardens and Fleet Street, Cheapside was an area of London closely associated with trade and shopping. Most of the city's merchants were found in these areas

coaching inn ~ hotel/pub/restaurant posted along major roadways that serviced the stagecoaches

Curzon Street ~ very wealthy (in Mayfair)

Fleet Prison ~ prison near the Fleet River for debtors and bankrupts

Gretna Green ~ town in Scotland just over the border from England where couples often eloped. A marriage could be obtained without a license, a clergyman, a waiting period, or parental consent; the couple only had to declare their intention to marry in front of witnesses

Harley Street ~ where many physician's set up residence

Hyde Park ~ an almost 400-acre park located in London's elite West End. 5:00 p.m. was the 'fashionable' hour to both see and be seen promenading along the man-made pond–called the Serpentine—or driving their fanciest carriage around the graveled pleasure-driving roads. This was known as the Ring. Rotten Row was the stretch of road notorious for speed demons –either horseback or carriages. For women, the park had the Ladies' Mile

in the busy expanse of Piccadilly

Kings Cross Station ~ London

Ladies' Mile ~ in Hyde Park

London Medical School for Women

London was at its peak

London's elusive West End ~ rich

London-town

Mayfair ~ the most desirable neighborhood in Regency London, located by Hyde Park

Mount Street ~ a narrow street lined with rows of elegant houses

Newgate ~ most formidable prison in London for criminals

Park Lane ~ in Mayfair

Parliament ~ the House of Commons and the House of Lords; always adjourned on August 12, the opening of the grouse season. Everyone headed north and the elite deserted London come August

River Thames flowed swiftly past

St. James Palace ~ home of the British monarchy during the Regency period

Tattersall's Repository ~ London's premier auction venue for bloodstock, horses; established in 1773 near Hyde Park Corner for the *sale/auction* of horses, carriages, hounds, harnesses, etc. since gentlemen vied with one another in being well-mounted; members of the *ton* drove in stylish carriages. When there were no sales, it was a fashionable lounge for sporting gentlemen. The Jockey Club's headquarters was there. Subscribers paid one guinea per year. All sporting bets were settled there, regardless of where the event took place

the Foundling Hospital

The Lamb and Flag ~ on Rose Street by Covent Garden; Charles Dickens a regular drinker here; since 1772 in London's infamous West End; known for its bare-knuckle fighting, it earned the nickname 'The Bucket of Blood'

the playground of princes and parliamentarians (Walton Heath/England)

the rolling hills of Surrey

the royal apartments of the Tower

the Royal Exchange and the Bank of England in the heart of London's financial district

Town ~ with a capital T, always refers to London

tyke ~ someone from Yorkshire

Vauxhall Gardens ~ pleasure garden of fountains, pavilions and walkways located across the Thames from fashionable London; offered entertainments such as dancing, elaborate fireworks displays, and music. Numerous dark walks proved suitable for assignations

Westminster Abbey ~ beautiful church; final resting place of kings and queens

U. Gentlemen's Clubs

~

became a popular fixture at White's

believe we have a table at Brook's waiting for us

Boodle's ~ founded 1762, St. James Street; founded by Lord Shelburne, the future Marquess of Lansdowne and Prime Minister of the United Kingdom. Club came to be known after the name of its head waiter, Edward Boodle. During the Regency era, Boodle's became known as *the* club of the English gentry, while White's became the club of the more senior members of the nobility. Boodle's is regarded as one of the most prestigious clubs in London, and counts many British aristocrats and notable politicians among its members.

Boodle's is the second oldest club in the world, with only White's being older

Brook's ~ founded 1762, St. James Street

East India Club ~ St. James Square

games of whist, faro, and hazard at Whites

Lord *whomever* was a member of Brooks'

The Carlton Club ~ founded 1832, St. James Street

The Garrick Club ~ founded 1831, Garrick Street

The In and Out, Naval and Military Club ~ St. James Square

The Reform Club ~ founded 1832, Pall Mall

The Travellers Club ~ founded 1819, Pall Mall

White's ~ founded 1736, St. James Street; oldest of the gentlemen's clubs; grew out of White's Chocolate House, which opened in 1698

White's was crowded with influential men of the beau monde

V. Working Class/Lower Class Professions

~

a yeoman warder at the Tower of London

actresses on Regent Street

apothecary ~ health practitioner who uses only herbal remedies; early version of a pharmacist

as the droning of the solicitor's voice washes over her

barrister ~ a lawyer who argues cases in court; they are hired by solicitors rather than direct clients. In England, Wales and Northern Ireland, this used to be the only type of lawyer qualified to argue a case in both higher and lower law courts; contrasts with *solicitor*. For Scotland, see Advocate.

Bow Street Runners ~ paid finders of criminals, housed on Bow Street in Henry Fielding's house

butchery ~ slaughter house

chemist ~ pharmacy, pharmacist

clergyman ~ Church of England, Anglican

constable ~ police officer/lower rank

costermonger ~ seller of fruits and vegetables/street vendor

draper ~ fabric store; someone who deals in clothing, textiles

dress shops stocked with the latest fashions

East India Company ~ powerful trading company that ran India for the British Empire. It was a lucrative career for second sons, but who got the best jobs was subject to the man's social standing or connections. Merchant ships that carried cargo/passengers between India and England were called East Indiamen. The company had docks and warehouses in London on the Thames

estate agent ~ someone who sells property, real estate for you

greengrocer ~ someone who sells fruits and vegetables

haberdasher ~ a dealer in small items and accessories, as for sewing; *haberdashery*

haberdashery ~ merchant shop that sells buttons, ribbons, threads, lace, and other trimmings for clothing. Sometimes this included such items such as reticules, gloves, fans, bonnets, etc.

high street ~ primary business and shopping street

inspector ~ police, lowest supervisory rank above sergeant, i.e. lieutenant

ironmongery ~ like a hardware store

keeper ~ a gaolkeeper

Master of Ceremonies ~ man at an assembly ball who announces which dance is next

military ~ relating specifically to the British Army

militia ~ army composed of regular citizens, not actual soldiers

milliner's shop ~ ladies' hat and bonnet shop that often sold ribbons, feathers, and artificial flowers for decorating your own hats

modiste/mantua maker ~ dressmaker

Partisan ~ yeoman warders at the Tower of London carry the staff made of solid oak; 18" blade

pressman/woman ~ a journalist employed by a newspaper

proctor ~ variant of the word procurator, is a person who takes charge or acts for another

solicitor ~ a lawyer who works closely with his client, not as formal as a barrister; lawyer who advises clients, represents them in the lower courts, and prepares cases for barristers to try in higher courts

street sweepers

surgery ~ the place where a physician or dentist practices, i.e. doctor's office

tradesman ~ a person who sells goods in a store

W. Extras

*~

'Stir-up Sunday' at the beginning of Advent

'til we find the blighter

"*Whoever*, I am not well; pray get me a glass of brandy."

1930s – had royalty serve as Captain at golf courses, i.e. King Edward was captain at Walton Heath golf course

a boy just out of short pants

a *by-blow of one of her many indiscretions/cad and a bounder*

a cake of soap

a *commodity of the marriage mart/grandiose affair*

a *delightful prattlebox/dreadful breach of etiquette*

a diamond of the first water ~ beautiful woman

a doxy whose favor he might perchance purchase

a gentle and loving person who treated everyone, no matter their title or position, with equal respect

a gentleman would lose his honor were he to 'cry off' a prospective marriage. A man's honor, in those days, was valued above everything—even happiness

a *gold-knobbed walking stick/rakish devil*

a hearty sound that

a knock sounded at the door, disturbing any further thoughts

a life *as a poor relation/of promise and prosperity*

a lord did not marry his lowborn mistress

a man's duty was to his crown and his family

a *mist of tears clouded her vision/prickle of unease crept down her spine*

a pattern-card of propriety

a *riding crop caught firmly beneath her arm/sturdy girl, not one given to vapors*

a scandal that would set all the *ton* on its ear, were it to become known

a *scoundrel of the worst sort/titled husband with plump pockets*

a significant difference in so-called love matches was that the upper class had to pick potential

a'tall

abbey ~ monastery

accomplishments ~ in keeping with the ornamental status of upper class women, an 'accomplished' young lady was expected to have cultivated talents such as playing the pianoforte, painting watercolors, speaking French, fancy sewing

act as my solicitor

alchemy

although they were almost of an age ~ the same age

altogethery

am certain the gossip mill will have run its course by then

an heir and a spare

an heir must be legitimate at birth to inherit a title (cannot be given or willed to a person later)

and then she run off ~ street language

and you think that signifies? ~ matters

announcements were more than likely not listed in newspapers, but may have appeared. Rumors of nuptials would be printed as well as caricatured in the press

apoplexy/apoplectic fit ~ in medicine, a stroke or cerebral hemorrhage. In general it refers to a fit of temper, rage

are queer in your attic

are you roasting me ~ teasing/kidding

are you witless enough to ~ if you are

arrogant blackguard!

as do I

as I recall

as if the closest of tie-mates

as you *please/were*

at all events ~ in any event

at sixes and sevens ~ muddled/in confusion/disarray

at the opera, a gentleman always escorted his lady in, walking side by side with her unless the aisle was too narrow. She took the inner seat, he the outer. A gentleman never left his lady's side from the beginning to the end of the performance. If she didn't wish to join the promenade at intermission, he remained with her in their seats

at *two-and-twenty/however much older than that*, she knew she was almost classified as being put on the shelf as a spinster

bachelor fare ~ woman of easy virtue

bah!

balderdash

Banbury stories ~ falsehoods

barely out of short dresses and braids

barmy ~ crazy/unbalanced

Bartholomew doll ~ the wooden dolls were called 'babies' instead of dolls until the 18th century

base born child ~ illegitimate

be off

become a tenant for life ~ marry

become quite the prattlebox

bedecked in

beg pardon, milady

beg to differ, dear boy

began to feel blue-deviled

being late to Almack's simply isn't done

Bell separated the portion of the work dealing with the fashions of the month from the remainder of the publication. For a time one could purchase either of the two divisions separately; the first consisting of the bulk of the magazine, together with two plates, the second ('La Belle Assemblée') consisting of the fashion plates and sewing pattern, together, usually, with four pages describing the plates and discussing the latest London and Paris fashions

bespoke ~ clothing made to the customer's specifications

betwattled ~ late 18th century Dorset British slang; confused, bewildered

Bird of Paradise ~ woman of easy virtue

bit o' muslin ~ woman of easy virtue

bits and bobs ~ odds and ends

bleeder ~ derogatory term for bloke

bluestocking ~ academic/smart woman

Bluestocking Society ~ informal group of society ladies began this movement in the 1750s to discuss literature and other educational matters as a revolutionary step away from the typical, acceptable activities of high class women

bone-idle ~ lazy

boorish cad

boot is quite on the other leg ~ situation reversed

bosh ~ nonsense

bother *and blast/it all*

botheration

bounder ~ an ill bred, unscrupulous man

brolly ~ umbrella

bugger off ~ go away/leave me alone

bum ~ a person's bottom

bumble-bath ~ clumsy/unwieldly

bumble-broth ~ make a mull of things

allowing him to take her arm and steer her effortlessly through the crowded room

but there was nothing for it ~ nothing he could do about it

by all that's blue

by Jove!

by Jupiter, I believe

by no means a nonesuch ~ an unrivalled thing/a paragon

by the by

capital news

capital, old friend

carriageway ~ portion of the road that carries the traffic

carried himself as a noble

carte-blanche ~ an offer to be kept by a gentleman, not marriage

cast up his accounts ~ vomit

Catherine Hutton—notable contributor to *La Belle Assemblée*

chaps ~ friends

chat up ~ talk flirtatiously with someone

chatelaine ~ the keys of authority at her waist

cheeky ~ impertinent

cheerio ~ informal way of saying farewell

cheers ~ informal way of saying thank you, or on parting (England)

children of a deceased father were subject to six-months of deep mourning

chin wag ~ chat

chit ~ young foolish girl

chuffed ~ pleased/proud/satisfied

Church of England required the reading of marriage banns for three consecutive Sundays, but this could be circumvented by getting a special license from the Archbishop of Canterbury, a procedure which men of means often used. This could be obtained at some considerable expense at the archbishop's office in Doctors' Commons in London

cit ~ contemptuous term for members of the working class

clodpole ~ stupid fellow, a dolt

cock sure ~ proud and confident

cock up ones toes ~ die

colleywobbles ~ stomach pain or queasiness

coming out ~ a lady's first entry into Society, must first be presented at court to the Queen

consumption ~ tuberculosis

coriander ~ the leaves of the coriander plant, cilantro

Corinthian ~ fashionable man about town

cork-brained ~ foolish/stupid

corn ~ wheat in England, oats in Scotland and Ireland

could *ill-afford to/scarce chide her for*

coxcomb ~ a man who effects extreme elegance in clothes and manners

coz ~ cousin

cross as crabs ~ ill tempered

current drama of the crown

cut direct ~ a deliberate and public snub

cut up my peace ~ disturb me

daft ~ odd/eccentric/crazy

dandy ~ a man who affects extreme elegance in clothes and manners; a fop

danger afoot

dashed bad luck for the groom to see the bride before the ceremony

decadence abounded, gambling was nearly a requirement, drinking in excess was expected, prostitution flourished, adultery was overlooked and violence was the norm

demimonde ~ class of women who were considered glamorous and possibly rich, such as actresses, but were far from respectable, mistress

demi-rep ~ woman of easy reputation

demmed ~ darned

despite his muddleheaded notions

destined to be one of the diamonds of the Season

diamond of the first water ~ a beautiful young woman

did not suffer skimble-skamble comments well

did not wish to vex

did she have attics to let?

didn't *come from gentry/feel utterly gauche*

dissenters ~ members of Protestant churches other than the Church of England, i.e. Baptists, Methodists, Quakers

do my ears play me false?

do not be a peagoose

do not be in a pelter ~ a passion, a fit of anger

do not *cosset her/say me false*

do tell. Do tell. (So you say.)

do you not mean shot by Cupid's arrow

do you think me a complete flat ~ lacking interest or imagination

do you wish me happy or

do, pray, be serious

dock ~ water between or next to a pier or wharf

don't be a ninnyhammer

don't be a widgeon ~ fool/simpleton

don't be so Friday-faced ~ sad looking

don't behave so missishly with me

don't blame you a'tall

don't fidget yourself ~ worry

don't want to spend another day without you in my life

done up ~ to be ruined by gambling

dovecote ~ small house, usually a circular tower shape, for doves and pigeons to nest in

draw someone's cork ~ punch in the nose and cause it to bleed

drawstring purse

drollery ~ whimsical humor/the act of jesting

ducedly handsome

dudgeon ~ bad mood

dunderhead ~ blockhead/dunce/numbskull

during deep mourning—six months after a husband died—social activities were curtailed for the family; the widow and other family members didn't go out in public or entertain beyond simple visits in their home

during the next period of mourning—the second six months of the year of mourning—widows were allowed to relax somewhat and add trims such as lace to the clothing to their clothes; could also add a few other colors such as lavender—which were still to be trimmed with black

each issue of La Belle Assemblée typically contained five plates—one depicting a member of the court or fashionable society, two depicting the latest fashions, and a further two providing sheet music and a sewing pattern

earbobs

educating women is a waste of money

effcte, pampered suitors

egad/egads, must you

elegance and grace

ended up on the edge of a scandal

engagements ~ were short; a wedding could take place within one month of the couple's initial *declaration/announcement*

entail ~ referring to property, meaning a landed estate was tied up in such a way it could be passed to one's heir after the owner's death, but the heir couldn't sell the property; limited where family inheritances go, usually went to a male

entirely besotted

every man jack of us

excellent waters at the Pump Room, I am certain of effecting a complete cure ~ Bath

expectations ~ the privileged members of the *ton* could pursue an opulent, extravagant life of indulgence, yet double standards for its members often existed. The flexibility of social rules was determined by an individual's status, wealth, or family connections

fancy ~ exhibit a fondness or preference for something

fashion, etiquette, manners, social customs, and other aspects of social life were all dictated by the *ton*. As London's most exclusive mixed-sex social club, Almack's represented the best and wealthiest

fashionable impures ~ rich mistress/prostitute/courtesan

fetch

fettle ~ condition

fighting for our Mother England

fighting the night phantoms

fire brigade ~ fire department

flambeaux ~ flaming torches

flannel ~ a cloth for washing the face or body; washcloth

flippin experts at it here

flowers ~ white corn-daisies and purple heartsease

fondness for the gaming dens

footpad ~ thief

fop ~ a dandy

for a long time he remained silent, rubbing his thumb over the back of her hand

found his feelings ran deeper than he expected

fratching ~ arguing/quarrel

free-traders ~ smugglers

French letter ~ condom

fresh out of university, he

frigate ~ common, three-masted, square-rigged sailing vessel designed for speed; often used as Navy warships or by privateers

fringe ~ bangs (hair)

frog ~ French person

fustian nonsense ~ rubbish

g'night

gads, no

gaol ~ jail

gave them the vapors

genteel young ladies rarely engaged in premarital sex; were shielded from sex

gentle as any maid-in-waiting, he

Gentleman Jackson ~ *boxing/pugilism* was wildly popular with all classes of men–as a spectator sport and an athletic hobby. Professional boxers didn't wear gloves and fought until one of the contenders couldn't get up off the ground. Gentleman Jackson was the reigning prizefighting champion from 1795 to 1818; he opened a boxing studio where he taught gentlemen 'the manly art of self-defense'

gentlemen's weapons ~ dueling pistols

gob ~ mouth

gobsmacked ~ astonished

gormless ~ stupid or clumsy

gossipmongers

grouse ~ game bird similar to a pheasant or quail that lives on the moors and is a favorite target for shooting; dogs retrieved the bird once it had been shot

growing physical awareness

had a fiercesome reputation

had never planned a tryst with a man

had taken a tidy sum to hush the gossips

harridan ~ bad-tempered, disreputable woman

has been much prattle about ~ talk at length in a foolish or inconsequential way

haven't a jot of color

havey-cavey ~ suspicious

he added in a low, tender tone

he *could think of nothing save her touch when/craved to touch her*

he forebore, however

he *was too handsome by half/weathered that scandal very well*

headache powders

held within his arms, she lost all rational thought

her *bounder of a husband/coming nuptials*

her first cousin, who would become the 6th Duke of *Wheverever*, became

her name on the London/New York social register

hire ~ to borrow for a set period of time, rent

hols ~ short for holiday

honor ~ the important principle/ideal behind gentlemanly or ladylike behavior

hoop skirts and landed gentry

house of cards

how vexatious

hoyden ~ mischievous girl who lacks decorum

I cannot abide

I collect you have ~ I assume

I could do with a good nosh up ~ big meal

I daresay

I *daresay/declare*,

I did not give you leave to use my Christian name

I didn't mean to lie abed so late

I expect ~ I guess

I fancy there's a mystery in it

I find that passing strange

I have just the dandy

I hope one day he comes by his desserts

I like to visit town occasionally, but it would not suit me to be forever there. I am happier here than

I meant no insult

I must own that *it/she* ~ admit

I offer you felicitations, sir

I own *I am pleased you/that I am quite surprised myself, but*

I own, I was very much

I plight unto thee my troth

I really must beg to be excused

I say, *whoever*, I asked you a question

I shall not be bound to accept an offer from a gentleman I cannot abide every day for the rest of my life

I suffered no insult

I tried, but he wouldn't have it

I wish you happy

I'd be beholden

I'll warrant I am

I'm beginning to believe you do not esteem my good company

I'm in no mood to go to a ball tonight

I've a notion it wasn't

if I may be so bold

if the *ton's* on-dits could be believed

ill suits you

illegal for a man to marry his deceased wife's sister

in future *I/we* shall

in good time, m'lord

in her youth she had been a beauty and the toast of her year

in his suddenly too tight breeches

in the event, it is

in the Regent's case, he had never met the cousin he wed until the actual wedding ceremony

indeed?

interestingly, neither

interval ~ break between two performances or sessions, as in theatre, intermission

introductions ~ a new person to a *party/gathering* was always introduced by someone that knew *him/her*. The new person would curtsey or bow; handshaking was reserved for true friends. Self-introductions were allowed by people of higher rank, but those of lower rank had to wait. They had to remain silent in mixed-rank company until an introduction was made. Once introduced to someone, it was expected they forever acknowledge that person with a bow, curtsy, or nod

is perchance the only

isn't pressing his suit

it does not signify ~ matter

it is not as if she intended to parade her on the marriage market

it is not like we are cits

it is *simply not to be borne/time and past that you*

it might be prudent

it simply would not do

it was *dashed strange, considering/not to be borne/quite of the first stare*

it was *half one when she/unseemly*

it was unlawful in England for a woman to marry her deceased husband's brother

it wasn't like her to be so churlish

jackanapes ~ rude or mischievous person, a knave

jobbernowl ~ numskull/nincompoop

jolly ~ very, i.e. jolly good

just ~ barely, i.e. I survived, but just

just so ~ right/yes, i.e. just so, sir

just sod off ~ leave it alone

keen ~ eager or intent on, i.e. he is keen on

kerfuffle ~ a disorderly outburst, disturbance

kick up a lark ~ get into mischief

kip ~ sleep/nap

knackered ~ broken/exhausted

knee deep in the doldrums

lack of social status

Lady Patronesses of Almack's during the Regency included Lady Jersey, Lady Sefton, Lady Cowper, Lady Castlereagh, and Mrs. Drummond Burrell

ladybird ~ a man's lover/mistress

lawks ~ (among cockneys) vulgar way to express surprise, awe

least those ~ at least those

leave be

let ~ to rent out

liberal ~ a person who generally supports the ideas of the UK Liberal Democrats, a centre left-party

life is hardscrabble

life revolved around society, the parties and balls given by *London's/New York's* élite

lift ~ elevator

like *some threepenny strumpet/unschooled hoydens*

liquor ~ broth resulting from prolonged cooking of meat or vegetables

littered with the crème de la crème of society

lived by the rigid rules of behavior

livery stable ~ stable where one could rent carriage horses. Could also board horses at a livery stable in London or, rent a horse to ride

loo ~ bathroom

looked *as straight-laced and prim as ever/like a Bartholomew doll*

Lord *whoever*, a word

lorry ~ a truck carrying goods

love matches were definitely the norm in the Regency but weren't the same as today's

love/luv ~ informal term of affection

loved the up-do

lud ~ polite *exclamation/way* of saying Lord

Lud, *child/no (Lord)*

luv

m'dear/father/whoever

mac ~ raincoat (Mackintosh)

make a mull of something ~ make a mess of

make an offer ~ propose marriage

make/making a cake of *myself/oneself* ~ make a fool of oneself

mark me ~ I'm sure

marriage agreements would specify how much 'pin money; the bride would receive annually from her husband

marriage licenses ~ *regular license* ~ when banns have been read as proscribed–three consecutive weeks–a regular marriage license would be granted. The marriage has to take place in one of the parish churches the betrothed couple belongs to, between the hours of 8:00 a.m. and noon; *special license* ~ way preferred by aristocrats was to purchase a special license from the offices of the Archbishop of Canterbury in Doctor's Commons in London. The specialmarriage license gave the betrothed couple the luxury of being married quickly, anywhere they wanted, and at any time of the day. Both types of licenses expired after three months

marriage mart

masque ~ costume ball

mate ~ friend

mawkish ~ sentimental

may I be the first to wish you happy

megrims ~ the blues/depression

mentioned in despatches ~ decorated for bravery in action

mercy, but

might do ~ I might

missish ~ *prim/prudish* behavior befitting a young miss

moggie ~ non-pedigree cat

moot ~ debatable, i.e a moot point

more's the pity

most often the girl would bring a dowry

mum ~ mother

must be devilish unnerving

must speak with him posthaste

naff off ~ get lost/go away

nappy ~ diaper

natter ~ idle, pleasant chatter

naught but a bloated tick on a hound's hide

nerves were frayed

ninnyhammer ~ fool

no disrespect intended

no easy task, that

no trims or decorations were allowed on dresses of widows for a year after the husband's death

no, I fancy not

no, nothing of import

nodcock ~ scatterbrain

nonetheless

nor ~ neither

nor did they deign to

not at all the thing

not *caring one whit about convention/feeling quite the thing this morning* not going to hide you away as a poor relation

not if it pains you, sir

not like the prancing popinjays she'd met and rebuffed in London

not *sounding a whit sorry for it/worth getting thrown into Newgate over*

nothing *but a rotter and a libertine/for it, then*

odd fish ~ someone regarded as eccentric or crazy and standing out from a group

of a sudden ~ suddenly

of all the crack-brained notions

of an age with her ~ same age

of doughty character ~ fearless, dauntless, determined

oh for pity's sake

oh, bosh ~ nonsense

oh, *bother/I say/rot*

oh, fustian! ~ rubbish

oh, so this is tit for tat? ~ equivalent retaliation

oh, the devil to pay

oh, the man was vexing

old chap

on the shelf ~ beyond a marriageable age/a spinster

once settled amidst the elegance

on-dits ~ piece of gossip/vague rumour

oughtn't ~ shouldn't

paragon ~ one of correct behavior and integrity

parasol ~ small umbrella for ladies to keep the sun off them

passing furious

peagoose ~ silly female

perish the thought

persnickety ~ fastidious

pig-widgeon ~ simpleton

pish *tosh/posh* ~ nonsense

pistols and rapiers

plait ~ braid hair

plaster ~ an adhesive bandage placed on a minor cut or scrape (UK also: *sticking/sticky plaster), i.e.* band-aid

pon my rep ~ a polite explanation

poppet

positively scandalous

post ~ to send a letter

post/postal box ~ mailbox

powdered wigs with tightly rolled curls at the temples that the English found so fashionable

preferred a yielding female to one taken by force

proper ~ real, or very much something, i.e. he's a proper hero

provisions in the marriage contract would be made for the wife in the event of her husband's death

pugilist

punch-up ~ fistfight

quaint, shady streets

queue ~ a line of people

quieten ~ quiet down

quite ~ well done, i.e. quite good

quite beyond the pale ~ an action that's regarded as outside the limits of acceptable behaviour, one that's objectionable or improper

quite right, old chap

quite *right/so*

quite so, quite so

quite the staid and decorous household

rain stinging against her face

rake ~ man with many vices; no doubt ruined many a woman

randy ~ having sexual desires/sexually aroused

really, it is beyond the pale

recollect that ~ don't forget that

reel of cotton ~ spool of thread

Regency brides didn't receive engagement rings

roads went to pudding

roast ~ to severely reprimand

row ~ a heated, noisy argument

rules for mourning were more lenient for men, who needed to be able to conduct business. Although some did wear all black—although it wasn't expected—most wore black armbands, black gloves, and in some cases, black cravats. The mourning period was also shorter for men

sailors, stevedores, and lightermen

scandal ~ i.e. that of an esteemed lord marrying a commoner

scapegrace

seasoned rider that she was

send to Coventry ~ ostracize/shun

sent to Jericho ~ exiled/shunned/cast out

set your cap for someone ~ try to get them to marry you

shag ~ have sex

shan't I

she had one foot on the shelf ~ spinster

she shines everyone else down ~ most attractive

she's a tempting armful if I do say so myself

she's nothing to this family. Naught but an outsider imposed on us after the death of her family

sheltered young brides-to-be from Britain's 'Upper Ten Thousand' often thought themselves in love with gentlemen they scarcely knew. Men also became besotted over ladies with whom they had barely spoken during the Season

shop ~ store

should be nattered ~ fret/upset

should hate for him to be unable to collect his vowels

should I ring for refreshments?

side whiskers ~ sideburns

since Saturday last

since there was little opportunity for intimacies, lovelorn couples had to proclaim their marital intentions *before* being accorded the opportunity to initiate any intimacies

Sir Ross Cannon, the magistrate of the Bow Street Runners after Fielding

sleet ~ snow that has partially thawed on its fall to the ground

slug-a-bed

smashing

so late of an evening

sod ~ unpleasant person

sod off ~ go away

some of you, I own, are worse than others

sowed his oats with little discretion

spot on ~ exactly

stall ~ front seats of a theatre; orchestra

steady on, old boy

sticky wicket ~ a difficult situation

stinging rain whipped across her face

stone ~ 14 pounds in weight, normally used when specifying a person's weight, i.e. four stone five (61 lbs)

straight away ~ immediately, right away

suss out ~ to figure out

swept her *a mocking/an elegant* bow

ta ~ British for thank you

tap ~ valve through which liquid is drawn and dispensed, i.e. faucet

tart ~ female prostitute

tatting was around during the Regency period

tea towel ~ a cloth used to dry dishes, cutlery, etc., after they have been washed

telly ~ television

tempting armful ~ attractive female

tend to irritate me by half

than any wish to respect the conventions of society

that *arrogant peacock/straitlaced old prig*

that bloke over there looks a bit dodgy ~ unsound/unstable/ unreliable

that *does not signify/had been too close by half*

that is a rum bit of luck ~ bad luck

that was a proper show

that's a fine kettle of fish

that's all gentlemen. Good day, ma'am

the brush of his lips demanding nothing

the cat's clearly got into the cream pot

the conventions of *ton* life were highly structured and complex. Crucial Social acceptance was primarily based on birth and family. Acceptable social behaviours were different for men and women; these were based on an intricate system validated primarily by the patronesses of Almack's, who determined who could be admitted to the club's functions. Some of these behaviours were flexible– they adapted slightly with the fashions of each season, and always reflected the current modes of manners, fashion, and propriety

the Countess of *Wherever*

the daily post ~ mail

the devil to pay ~ trouble

the *dizzying social circuit/duke got kicked out of Almack's*

the earl was promoting this match

the foul-tempered blackguard

the idea was simply not to be borne

the *lamp cast uneven shadows/large, drafty house*

the lot of you ~ all of you

the picture of elegance and refinement

the pleasure was too exquisite to be borne

the pompous prig

the post road being in bad repair

the scandal of the divorce reached the gossip mills

the *stench which drifted up from the Thames/Thames waterman*

the toast of the *ton*

the topic of *whatever* thus dispatched ~ ended

the *unwanted stirring in his loins/worst of libertines*

the wind tore her hair loose from its once neat knot

the young *lady acts the hoyden/swain was quite foxed*

then they are widgeons

there is nothing else for it

there was a scandal, I collect ~ I remember

there was nothing for it but to wait, though

there was nothing for it, then

these *however many* months past

they must be of an age

they're quite the thing

this is most untoward

this was the woman with which he would willingly leg-shackle himself

throng ~ crowd

throw a wobbly ~ lose one's temper

throwing a rub in the way ~ to spoil plans

time *she made her bow to Society/to beget an heir. You have a duty to your family*

tim-whiskers

titillating gossip

to be sure ~ certainly

too clever by half

took the ball and reeled ~ gunshot

tooth powder, shaving brush, razor strap

tosh ~ nonsense

tower/tower block ~ a fortified keep, too small to be named a castle

trapped by the worst of the town tabbies

trice ~ in a moment/very quickly

trying to jest her out of her dismals ~ hopeless/sad mood

turned a baleful eye on

tussie-mussie ~ a small bunch of flowers or herbs

two hunting hounds snarled over a bone

unbefitting your station

unholy interests ~ gay

utter rot

vapors ~ hysterics

very astute of you, my lord

very good, my lord

viewed him as if he were a candidate for Bedlam

vowels ~ betting IOUs

want-wit ~ fool

want-witted ~ senseless

was a bit of a prattle-box

was a diamond of the first water

was a war veteran and fiercely loyal to the crown

was an incorrigible scapegrace

was beyond the pale, even for him

was common to marry first cousins

was going to drive him straight to Bedlam

was no lady's maid

was simply not good form

wedding breakfast

well then, there is nothing for it

what a bumble-bath

what a *fine fettle this was turning out to be/want-witted scheme*

what Banbury tale would he tell next

what ho! ~ hello

what is amiss

what side of the blanket one is born on

what the deuce was she doing traveling alone

what trickery is this

what you want does not signify

whatever are you on about

whatever color curls spilling from the *kerchief/mobcap*

when he had been so top over tail in love ~ i.e. head over heels

when their 'pockets are to let' they may turn to 'parson's mousetrap' to restore their funds

when they told me *whatever*, I thought they were having me on

when you hear the tower bell

whence hail you

whilst ~ while

who had sat opposite her in the mail coach

who might be late. And not only entry for tonight. Many a society climber had lost their place by ~ Almack's

who wasn't as much of an heiress as he needed to wed. His lavish lifestyle had put him in debt

whopstraw ~ clod-hopper

why are you in a pelter?

why it would be an unsuitable match

why would I buy old boots ~ marry another man's mistress

why would I do something as skimble-skamble as that? ~ rambling or confused/senseless

widows expected to wear black for a year after their husbands died

without a jot of mercy

women not permitted to be alone with gentlemen

would never be a darling of the *ton*

yank ~ someone from the US

yes, my lord

you are in a pelter ~ angry

you don't look all the thing

you go too far, *my lord (or whoever)*

you know dashed well we're

you libertine ~ a person, especially a man, who behaves without moral principles or a sense of responsibility, especially in sexual matters

you must ask him, I daresay

you need to be aware that someone might wish you ill

you only wear a tiara if you're married

you popinjay ~ a vain or conceited person, especially one who dresses or behaves extravagantly

you properly bodged that up ~ made a mess of it

you put me in an untenable position, my lord

you're getting yourself in a taking ~ upset

you're talking codswallop ~ nonsense

young women simpering and preening

Add Your Own Regency Tags!

*~

Add Your Own Regency Tags!

*~

2

MEDIEVAL ~ SCOTTISH ~ IRISH

A. Medieval

*~

1) Dwellings/Furnishings

*~

a *few embers still glowed on the hearth/torch blazed in its bracket*

accessed the room by means of a hidden passage

all around them, the castle's outer bailey hummed with activity

arrow *slits/loops* ~ slots in the *walls/structures* used to shoot arrows through. Came in a wide variety of shapes and sizes

bailey ~ courtyard or open space surrounded by walls

barbican ~ stone structure that protected the castle gate. Usually had a small tower on each side of the gate where guards stood watch

bare feet slapping against cold stone

bastion ~ tower or turret projecting from a wall, or at the junction of two walls

battlements ~ structures at the tops of the walls surrounding a castle. Allows archers to fire arrows between open slots down on oncoming attackers

beds used by the poor were called pallets/trundles; mattresses were made of straw

burst through the door of the keep

bustling courtyard

buttress ~ masonry projection used as additional support for walls

candlelight flickered off the stone walls

canopied/hung beds were a status symbol of wealthy nobles. The base of the bed had a wooden frame with holes in it. Rope was pulled through these holes in a criss-cross pattern which formed the base of the bed. Mattress usually made of feathers and placed on top of the base. The bed canopy assemblage consisted of a bed head, or tester, rising to a suspended frame, which was covered and draped in fabric. The bed would have sheets, quilts, fur coverlets, and pillows. The whole bed could be enclosed by curtains. The four-poster bed was eventually a requirement of every Medieval Lord

carpets and mats were rarely used; straw or rushes were more common

chairs in the Great Hall were considered a luxury and wooden benches were more commonly used to sit on. Trestle tables were used for dining

chests used for traveling were designed without feet or legs

chests with permanent places in the castle had legs, which kept the chest off the filthy rushes and sometimes vermin infested castle floors. These heavier chests also tended to be more ornate

climbed the spiraling stairwell

corbel ~ stone projection from a wall that supports the weight of a battlement

courtyard ~ (aka ward) open area within the curtain walls of a castle

covering the opposite wall was a tapestry

crenellations ~ same as battlements

crowds were thinning as the tradesmen closed their stalls for the day

curtain wall ~ stone walls around a castle; the castle's first line of defense

donjon ~ old word for a great tower/keep

drawbridge ~ wooden bridge in front of the castle's main gate. In early centuries of castles it moved horizontal to the ground; in later centuries it raised up in hinged fashion

dungeon ~ deep dark cell, typically underground and underneath a castle

embrasure ~ opening in a parapet wall

fire blazing in the upstairs hearth

footway ~ sidewalk

frenzied voices erupted from the great hall below

fresh rushes covered the hard earthen floor

from where they stood she could see many merlons on the battlements had

front parlor, dining room, and a kitchen with cupboards a circular stone stairway swept up to the (wide steps)

furniture was assembled with joints secured by wooden pegs or iron nails. Glue was used to fasten canvas or leather which sometimes was added as an exterior finish or lining

gate house ~ fortified main entrance to a castle. May have a guard house or living quarters

glass slickstone to do laundry

great hall ~ major area inside the walls of a castle where meals were eaten and festivities held; also frequently served as the lord's office, a meeting hall where courts and other functions were held

grianon ~ women's sun room

guards kept watch on the roof and parapet

guests and castle folk slept in the Great Hall when bed chambers were full

heads appeared on the palisades

hieburde ~ top table in the Great Hall

high, timbered ramparts

his steward

hoarding ~ covered wooden gallery above a tower; floor had slats/slots to allow defenders to drop liquid/objects on besiegers

hurried *across the muddy courtyard/along the parapets, staring out to sea*

hurried down the staircase, *whoever* on his heels

hurried down the *stone steps, shouting out orders/winding steps of the turret*

ill-lit *corridors/hallways*

items used to cover furniture included: leather, tapestry work, velvet

ivy covered ruins

keep ~ where the laird and his family lived. The main tower this area was built around was usually the tallest and strongest structure in the castle; also used as the last line of defense during siege or attack

lady of the castle an expert at needlework

lit a branch of candles

machicolations ~ a floor opening between the corbels of a parapet. They form areas that stick out along the top of the wall and defenders can drop items like boiling oil or rocks onto attackers at the base of a defensive wall

merlons ~ parts of parapet walls between embrasures

moat ~ water surrounding the outer wall of a castle, often around 5 to 15 feet deep. Sometimes it was within the outer wall—between the outer and inner wall. A moat made access to the walls difficult for siege weapons, such as siege towers and battering rams. They not only helped to stop attackers, they also stopped tunnelers. Tunneling under a castle was an effective means of collapsing the walls or infiltrating it

most of the tables were trestle-tables, which enabled quick removal after the meal to make room for entertainment or for servants to sleep

motte and bailey ~ early form of castle where a large mound of dirt was built up, then a wooden or stone fortification was placed on top. This fortification was in the shape of a timber fence that formed a circle at the top of the mound. The earthen mound is the motte, and the timber structure and the space it enclosed is the bailey

murder hole ~ opening in the roof of a gateway over an entrance, used to drop projectiles or other things onto besiegers

narrow slit-like windows

punctuated the wall

oubliette ~ deep pit reached by a trap door at the top where prisoners were kept

once outside the gates

oratory was used as a private chapel and would have an altar

oriel window ~ window that sticks out from a building. Made of stone or wood and often had corbels underneath to support them

oval mirror of hammered silver

palisade ~ defensive fence

picked up the slickstone and smoothed it over the heavy silk carefully ~ iron

portcullis ~ metal or wooden grate that was dropped vertically just inside the main gate to the castle

postern ~ small gate at the back of a castle

rampart ~ defensive wall of a castle or walled city, having a broad top with a walkway and a stone parapet. This walkway/rampart was built flush against the outer wall

red and green were the most popular colours used to paint furniture, but white, yellow, and black were also used. It was fashionable to paint heraldic designs on special pieces of furniture belonging to the *laird/lord* of the castle

retreated to her bedchamber

rolling land around the castle

rushes crunched beneath her bare feet

sconces lit the room

she reached up and pulled one of the torches from its sconce

sleeping mats

slept on pallets in the hall

slept on shake downs in the Great Hall when no chambers were available

snores of the garrison

solar was used for sleeping and as private quarters by the Lord's family. Also a private sitting room favoured by the family. Furniture included beds, chairs and chests

some wealthy *lairds/lords* had chairs with high straight backs and seats and arms, sometimes stuffed with rushes

stairwells in medieval castles were narrow and curved clockwise. Attackers coming up the stairs had sword hands—if right handed—against the interior curve of the wall and made it very difficult to swing their swords. Defenders had their sword hands on the outside wall, giving them much room to swing

stood in the Great Hall, his feet planted upon the rushes

strode over to the bow window

sweet smelling herbs such as chamomile, daisies, fennel, lavender, and rose petals were sprinkled on rushes to disguise the bad smells of the castles

tapestries *graced the walls/taken down and beaten to clean them of dust*

tapestry curtains around the bed were drawn to keep out drafts

the bailey was alive with activity

the Bower was intended for the Lady of the castle and used as her private withdrawing room. Chests for garments, and a few benches and stools decorated the Bower

the captain of his men-at-arms

the deep rich tones of her laughter carrying across the hall

the *earthen floor/floor swept clean and new rushes put down*

the *fortress stood on the rise of a hill/gray stone keep*

the hall was huge, capable of entertaining more than a hundred people at a time

the long table where he sat alone breaking his fast

the lord's bed the most expensive piece of furniture in the castle

the high, crenallated walls

the hues of the tapestries dulled by age

the jongleurs, the acrobats, the minstrels/men and women who peopled its halls

the magnificent *dining hall/staircase*

the seneschals who related tales of courage and grandeur

threw *his reins to a waiting page/the castle gates wide in welcome*

thrones—for Kings and Queens—were usually cushioned, sometimes upholstered and elaborate chairs. The throne was placed on a dais under a canopy and accompanied by a footstool

to return to his own stronghold

torches flickered in iron torches affixed to the wall

towering stone tower

towers rose majestically

under cover of the forest

wall sconces held candles, giving a flickering glow to the large room and bringing out the richness of the velvet and brocade tapestries lining the walls

wall were high and thick

wardrobe was intended as a dressing/storage room for clothes of the *laird/lord*. This private room also became the storage area for costly items such as jewels, furs, coins, spices, and plates. Would be furnished with various chests and coffers

wheels creaked and hooves clattered as the entourage left the bailey

when the last of the odists finished souterrain ~ underground pantry (cut in the earth and lined with stone blocks to retain coolness)

where stately twin turrets stood guard like vigilant sentinels

woods used to build furniture were: oak, ash, beech, elm, and larch

yett ~ iron gates at the entrance of a castle

2) Swords/Fighting

~

a (*black*) sword solidified in his hands and the shimmery (*darkness*) moved *down/over/through* his body

a battle cry tore from his lips

a bloody struggle for survival

a fierce joy at finally fighting his enemy

a seasoned warrior

a host of war machines heading toward the castle

an *arrow knocked in place/unflinching warrior*

archers were in place, their bows at the ready

as well as lance and sword, they carried battle-ax, billhook, and iron ball-and-chain at their belts

attacked her father's palisade

axes at the ready

barrels of Greek fire ~ an incendiary device that could continue burning while floating on water

bashing his buckler into his face

battering rams and mangons

battle-scarred warrior

bayonet affixed to the musket

bayonet came into play in the 17th century

billhook ~ attached to a long pole

blade trailed fire

blinked down to see the gleaming white-gold hilt protruding from a sheath at his side

bore down on him with broadsword raised threateningly

brandished the dagger before jamming it beneath his belt

brandishing swords

Captain of the Guard

carried their spears couched under their arms

challenged, and he picked up the gauntlet

chopped a nearby tree to use as a battering ram

clad in leather pants and wore a weapons belt with a sword on one side and a dagger on the other

clashing swords

clenched his jaw and gripped the hilt of his sword

closed in on the fleeing enemy

could hear the hissing of the swords

countered with a swipe of the fiery golden sword

countering the blow

drew a sword and dispatched him with a single thrust

drew the sword away with a vicious wrenching twist, and its tip was coated in blood

drove a *sleáne* through his heart

every blow was dodged or deflected with dance like grace

fewtering his *weapon/spear*, he

fletchers making arrows

focusing on the imminent battle, blades clanged together

foot slipped, he fell-rolled recovered to find himself gazing over crossed swords

for the first time she noticed his sword was honed to a razor's edge

fought against Spain's attempts to overthrow the monarchy

freed his sword

Greek fire ~ an incendiary weapon developed ca. 672 and used by the Eastern Roman (Byzantine) Empire. The Byzantines typically used it in naval battles to great effect, as it could continue burning while floating on water

hand trembling, he touched the cool metal guard, closed his fingers around the handle, and drew the weapon slowly

he countered *the stroke/with his sword, slicing off a good portion of the other's shield*

he dodged another swinging chop from the other's mace and turned his horse away in a circle, coming up on the other side

held the sword, its weight felt alien, its hilt strange to him it fit his hand as if made for him, seemed to warm to his

his *attack as quick as a flash of lightning/forearms straining as he ruthlessly slashed*

his retinue

his sleeveless leather shirt showed his finely carved forearms, a light scattering of (*black/dark*) hair led down to strong hands

his sword brothers

his sword *sang from its sheath/slashed down*

hit the ground and sprang at once to his feet, drawing his sword and dodging two knights

hot pitch and boiling water splashed down on them

in battle he was fearless

it felt as if he'd held the gleaming weapon all his life. He knew he could wield it as if it were an extension of his arm

it was the color of purity, goodness and it gleamed

keep an eye out for sappers

lances outstretched before them

lifted a hand to his men

lifted the gleaming-white broadsword, now pulsing with *energy/ power* in his hand

many of the troops were inexperienced and lacked the training to stay in a straight line

marked their arrows

men he ate with, fought with, bled with

met him with a swift parry, neatly catching the blade and turning it aside

metal rang on metal

morningstar was a ball that had spikes all over it. Hung by a chain on the end of a pike or by something held in your hand

pledged his sword to him

pulled a dagger out of it's hidden (*place*) sheath at his waist

pushed the man away with all his strength

raised his hand, the air around them shimmered like heat waves

raised his shield and sent forth his battle cry

raised his sword in the opening salute. *En garde*

readied his sword and advanced on

rendered him unconscious with the hilt of his sword

repetitive blows to the shield, tiring him

rested a wary hand on the hilt of his sword

saw the sword flash leaving a glittering comet in its wake

shimmering sparks showed the path the sword had taken

slid his sword slowly into its scabbard

sprinted, sword in hand pouring every ounce of his strength into his stride

sprung to their feet, weapons drawn

steel rang on steel

sword *drawn/high in fury*

sword swinging, slicing—he didn't allow it to slow him

swords can sever an enemies' arm or lop off his head

swords touched as he turned the blade, watching it gleam

the archers' response quick and accurate

the *bow poised between two merlons on the walkway/burning arrows lit up the sky*

the art of wielding a broadsword against forces darker than midnight had become a part of who he was

the chink of the chain mail

the *clang of swords and shields/flashing of encrusted sword hilts*

the field surged with fighting men, some on horseback, some fighting on foot

the large battle axe arced out

the huge warhorse reared and snorted

the sounds of battle deafening

the swords flashed again and again, collided over and over, sending showers of fiery sparks into the air

the vibration of the first blow shot up his sword arm

they fought with great swings of their weapons, pounding one another

thread your arrows

threw himself into the heat of battle with abandon

trebuchet ~ a medieval military machine that hurled missiles (rocks, etc.); a beast of destruction

used a felled tree as a battering ram

used all of his skills to *defend while he was deep in thought/put his plan into effect*

waiting silently in the shadows, spears and shields in hand

warhorses snorting

warrior cut down in his prime

was sick of bloodshed for the sake of bloodshed

watched as many fell beneath the sword

watched him move with lethal grace and fluidity, his weapon an extension of his arm

whirled *around sword arm already in motion/at the sound of steel on steel*

wielded the sword with the skill of an expert

will also take a full complement of warriors to watch our backs walked across the sward

with *a single swipe he ripped through the force field/his mail coif, he was*

world of blood feuds and retaliation

you could die right here, bearing arms against the army of Her Majesty, the Queen

3) Clothing

~

a form-fitting bodice with an oval neckline edged in ecru lace that accented her slender, shapely figure beneath

a pale gown molded against enticing curves

a robe of heavy damask trimmed with fur

a *sgian dubh* tucked in the top of his tartan hose

after shaving, whoever donned a clean shirt

after smoothing out her skirt she

aghast at her boy's clothes

ancient plaide ~ laid his belt on the floor and placed his tartan atop it, lengthwise. Stretching out on it, he crossed the unpleated edges of the fabric across his middle and buckled it in place. Drawing the excess over his shoulder, he fastened it with the round brooch

arranged the skirts of her *any* colored gown

baldric

basic garments for women consisted of a smock, hose, kirtle, gown, surcoat, girdle, cape, hood, and bonnet

basque ~ close fitting waist-length jacket with a single row of buttons, long tight sleeves, and a short tail at the back

bedrobe ~ bathrobe

began untying the points of his braies

braies ~ a type of trouser worn by Celtic and Germanic tribes and by Europeans subsequently into the Middle ages; in the later middle ages they were used exclusively as undergarments

brown velvet

buckling his baldric across his chest

cape trimmed with ermine

cast aside her mantle and

changed into a simple frock

chemise, undertunic, and overtunic

clad in wolf skins and chain mail

clothes ragged and ill-fitting

clothing of the nobility was fitted, with an emphasis on the sleeves

clothing stained with travel

clothing varied according to the social standings of the people

coats and surcoats often trailed on the ground

collar turned up against the cool evening air

covered in rich furs

daywear: light muslin dresses decorated with their needlework

doublet

drew her rain sodden cape around her

female clothing consisted of two tunics, the under one being longer but less fancy than the other

frog

fur sporran

gambeson

garb yourself

grabbed him by his tunic front with lightning speed

helped him into his mail chausses and hauberk

her comely figure beneath her *whatever color* kirtle brought a smile to his *face/lips*

her fur trimmed tunic

her hair tucked away out of sight under a big white kerchief

his *cloak retrieved/clothes were none too clean*

his mantle lifted and blew behind him as he rode toward

hooded cloak

I'm probably going to have problems with the clothes

in a swirl of houppelande ~ an outer garment, with a long, full body and flaring sleeves, that was worn by both men and women in Europe in the late Middle Ages

indiscreetly adjusting his gambeson

knights wore sleeveless surcoats covered with a coat of arms

leather *garters/jerkin*

lifting one hand to steady her bonnet

light green merino pelisse

long sleeved undergown called a chainse, a shorter sleeveless gown over it unbelted ~ Saxons

mantle ~ long coat/cape with arm slits and a hood, i.e. long, satin, trimmed with marten

married women kept their hair covered with a scarf or headdress

materials used were woolen cloth, fur, and cambric; richer women wore silk and linen

men—regardless of social rank—wore a cloak, tunic, trousers, and leggings

nearly spilling from the confines of her tunic

only the wealthy could dress in fashionable clothing

peasant clothing very simple

picked up her skirts and hurried across the courtyard

points of snowy Irish lace at the collar and wrists

propped his foot on a stool near the hearth and began to unlace his brogues

pulled her cloak tighter, only her eyes and hands visible as she crouched out of sight

pulled off one boot, then the other, dropping them

removed his helmet, gambeson, mail shirt, and leather chausses

rose from the *chair/table/floor/ground* and smoothed her skirts

scantily dressed

shedding herself of her cape

shivering in her thin nightrail

shrugged off a heavy redingote

shucked off the last of his clothes

shucking off his coats and tossing them

silk jupon

straightened her skirt

straightened the collar on his suit coat

surcoat ~ a garment with an open bodice and a skirt that trailed to the ground

tabard ~ a short loose-fitting sleeveless or short-sleeved coat or cape; a tunic worn by a knight over his armor and emblazoned with his arms

the hem of his greatcoat whirling about his high, polished boots

the plumes on her bonnet bobbed

the soft rustling of her skirt

the soft soled shoe

the wet skirt clinging to her long shapely legs

their clothes the height of fashion

thin woolen cloak

tied the points on his gambeson

tiny emerald teardrops dangling from her ears

trews (truis/triubhas) ~ men's clothing for the legs and lower abdomen, a traditional form of tartan trousers from Scottish apparel. Trews could be trimmed with leather, usually buckskin, especially on the inner leg to prevent wear from horseback riding. Tartan trews shared the fate of other items of Highland dress, including proscription under the Dress Act of 1746 that banned men and boys from wearing them outside of military service. The Dress Act lasted until 1782 when it was repealed under the reign of King George III

tugged at her nightrail

tying his trews

unbuckled the clasp that fastened his baldric to his shoulder

unlaced his brogues

wearing *a mail hauberk over his gambeson/the latest fashion*

wearing a shift as underclothes, women wore a simple long dress, loosely cut to allow for pregnancy; it was fastened at the shoulders by a brooch

wearing a silk *whatever color* gown that clung to every curve of her body

what could she possibly do with all those clothes

whatever color houppelande with wide maunch sleeves covering a *whatever color* undertunic

women wore *closed shoes/long cloaks over their clothing*

women wore kirtles (tunics) to their ankles. These were often worn over a shirt

worried the fabric of her sleeve

you cannot get warm in sodden clothing

4) Drinking

*~

a 'butt' ~ medieval measurement for wine

a tankard of foaming mead

after dipping up cups of heather ale

ale and mead flowed freely

ales made from barley quaffed the thirst, as would water drawn from the well, sweetened with honey

could smell the mead on his breath

cupped her hand around her tankard

drink was flowing freely

everyone raised their cup in accord

holding a tankard aloft

in his drunken befuddled state

joined them in several rounds of *uisge beatha*

let's have a wee *toast/dram*

offering him the wineskin

quaffed down the last of his ale

quaffing ale and wolfing down meat pies

raised his tankard in a toast

sipped and put the tankard down silently

slammed his tankard of mead down on the table

stared morosely into the depths of his tankard

swigged from his tankard to ease the fever in his brain

swilling mead

tankard of ale

5) Foodstuffs

*~

ate cereals that were predominantly barley, oats, rye, wheat, and linseed based

ate pretty much any meats like: bear, beaver, chicken, cow, deer, duck, goose, hare, horse, rabbit, otter, pig. If they lived close enough to water to fish, they would also eat freshwater fish, oceanic fish, and seal

barley, oat and rye were prevalent among the poor

blancmange ~ aka shape, is a sweet dessert commonly made with milk or cream and sugar thickened with gelatin, cornstarch, or Irish moss and often flavored with almonds. It is usually set in a mold and served cold. Although traditionally white, blancmanges are often dyed with other colors. A similar dessert is Bavarian cream. Blancmange originated in the Middle Ages and usually consisted of capon or chicken, milk or almond milk, rice and sugar, and was considered to be an ideal food for the sick

breakfast wasn't eaten when people first got up in the morning. Several chores were done before they stopped to eat

breakfasts usually consisted of soup and grain products

broiled venison

butcher's meats were pork, chicken and other domestic fowl

cereals remained the most important staple

chicken pasties

civey of hare

cod and herring were mainstays among the northern populations

colewarts ~ a primitive cabbage

corn ~ wheat in England, oats in Scotland and Ireland

dairy products such as cheese and butter could be seen on tables of the wealthy

diet for peasants traditionally consisted mostly of pork, beans, cabbage, turnips, oats, cheese, eggs and rye or wheat bread

dinner – usually consisted of soup, bread and vegetables, followed by fish or meat

dried, smoked or salted, cod and herring sometimes made their way far inland, but a wide variety of other saltwater and freshwater fish was also eaten

eel pie

families lucky enough to get their hands on salt pork or fatty bacon would have added these to their soups for flavor

felled a stag and a wild boar this day

fish would either be sold fresh or smoked and salted

for the most part, meat was only for the wealthy

forks weren't used during the medieval period. Food was eaten with knives

fowl such as capons, geese, larks, and chickens were usually available only to the lord and his family

fruits like apples, pears, berries were eaten to add variety to the meals. Nuts were often added as well

honey and raisins often added to food to sweeten it

it was a status symbol to serve food with herbs and spices

kippers

manchet ~ a thick slice of day old bread made of wheat flour that served as a plate

meat acquired from hunting was common only on the tables of the nobility

meat was roasted, boiled, or baked in pies

mushroom pasties

Norman pasties

offering her only the choicest morsels

onions, cabbage, garlic, nuts, berries, leeks, spinach, and parsley were some of the foods that would be combined to make thick soup. Raw vegetables were considered unhealthy and rarely eaten, but anything that could grown, with the exception of known poisonous plants, were added to the mix

only ate two meals per day—breakfast and dinner

only lords and nobles were allowed to hunt deer, boar, hares and rabbits, so these foods were only used in the daily meals of the nobility

pandemain loaves and soft ruayn cheese

peasant breads were made from barley and rye, baked into dark heavy loaves

people enjoyed drinking, but since water was often unclean, it was more a necessity than a matter of drinking alcohol. The poor drank ale, mead or cider, while the rich were able to drink many different types of wines

plump, sweet rastons ~ sweet bread

pokerounce dripping with honey roast haunch of venison

potatoes and tomatoes weren't eaten then as they were thought to be poisonous. Potatoes weren't introduced until 1536

roast leeks with onions

salat ~ medieval salad

scones with marmalade

sipping on a skin of goat's milk

spices used by wealthy were anise, cardamon, caraway, cinnamon, cloves, coriander, cumin, garlic, ginger, mace, mustard, nutmeg, pepper, saffron, and turmeric

staple diet for lower classes were bread, pottage (a type of stew), dairy products such as milk and cheese products and meats such as beef, pork or lamb

staple diet of the lower classes were bread, pottage (a type of stew), dairy products such as milk and cheese products and meats such as beef, pork or lamb

supper - a light meal; food and drink generally served between 10:00-11:00—accompanied by various forms of entertainment

the upper and lower classes usually had three meals a day, but commoners ate far less elaborately than the upper classes

toward the end of the medieval period people started to eat lunch

trout with galentyne

vegetables were important supplements to the cereal-based diet of poorer classes

wealthy families dined on such meats as beef, bacon, lamb, and those living close to water may have regularly dined on salmon, herring, eels ands other fresh water fish

wheat for the governing classes, were eaten as bread, porridge, gruel and pasta

6) Things to Do/Chores

*~

bells calling the faithful to prayer

bows, bent and oiled regularly to keep them supple

called the command over his shoulder and raced down the hall

castle stewards bargained with traders over the price of

committed to the needs of his people

currying favor with their King

dismissed the guards with a nod

during practice in the lists

embroidered by her own hand

forces that had declared for *whoever/the queen* and were marching to join her

had drawn up his men in circular schiltrons

he adjusted the dagger he was never without into the sheath at his waist

his *order to be about her labors decisively curt/squire standing a pace or two behind him*

hone his skills

jongleur ~ an itinerant medieval entertainer proficient in juggling, acrobatics, music, and recitation the night candle flickering in the sconce on the wall

medieval embroidery

passing smiths and artisans

picked up the slickstone and smoothed it carefully over the silk

proudly upheld the vows of knighthood

raided the coasts of Albion

serfs were busy supplying the

servant came quickly from the shadows

sheep tallow soap

strumming lutes

sworn upon their spurs to protect women ~ knights

tenants came to renew their tacks (leases)

the *blacksmith's busy forging weapons of steel/lord was served first/next morning the headsman was waiting (beheading)*

tilted at the quintain

tournament/tourney ~ chivalrous competitions or mock fights of the Middle Ages/Renaissance

waved the servant away

7) Horses

*~

destrier was heaving with exertion

his destrier galloped forward

horses pounded into the foreyard of the castle

kneeing her steed forward

reined his charger to a halt

remounting his steed

turned his mount toward the castle

8) Medieval Extras

*~

a child was usually baptized on the day he was born

a woman's role was to support her husband

among the nobility and wealthier town folk, wet nurses were common

apprenticeships began in the teen years

babies clad in simple gowns

besotted with

bewail a fate that

Blanchette ~ Norman for white

blast her but she was stubborn

blessed mercy, ~ swearing

bound at neck and maunch by

but the tides of fortune weren't

by thunderation, I

can't you see she's with child?

catamites

catching *little/wee whoever* up in his arms

Cease!

childbirth the most common death for young women

children played with toys and simple games, playing ball or hoops, racing, chasing each other, climbing trees, walls and other structures, girls played with cloth dolls, and engaging their imaginations

children taught manners, personal hygiene, and skills necessary to survive in a hostile world and get along with their neighbors

Christ Mass celebrations

Christian banns had been cried

circle widdershins thrice

clenched his fists and swore a faerie oath that had the dryads in the hawthorn trees beside him peeking out from the branches in trepidation

could see afresh

current drama of the crown

daughters couldn't inherit land from their parents if they had any surviving brothers

departed the hall in angry strides

didn't make a habit of wenching

dissenters stripped of their wealth and holdings

draughts ~ checkers

eagerly opened the missive

entwined fish or birds ~ symbols which represent the union of celestial and earthly forces

ere ~ before

escorted by four of his most capable knights

eventide ~ evening

eyeing him balefully

eyes would meet across the banqueting table in the hall

fair maids

fearing the wrath of

fewter ~ a *support/holder* for a spear, attached to a saddle or breastplate

for non-wealthy children, learning how to do such simple tasks as carrying water, herding geese and gathering fruit would have begun at a young age

for the love of the Saints

forces encamped

forsooth

fortnight ~ two weeks

found himself fed, wined and wenched to his satisfaction

garotted

gave no quarter

girls from *wealthy/prominant* families usually married someone as a political gesture or because it was advantagous to the girl's family

girls had *no choice who they married/to have their parent's permission to marry*

girls taught spinning and needlework and other domestic skills to prepare them for marriage

give way

God and all the fairies must be smiling on him today

good day, my lord

guilds began to insist potential apprentices be able to read and write

guilty of treason against his king

had a fiercesome reputation

had *her back flogged to ribbons/ tired of bloodletting*

halberd

hanging from the gibbet

hard callouses marked his palm, testimony to his skill as a knight

he *despoiled her/forebore, however*

he hides behind *Alfred's/whoever's* robes at court

heed me, have a care what you say

heading for the hall with her head high

henceforth you will not

her betrayal had *sliced/cut* deeper than any *blade/dirk/sword/knife*

her *fists beating against his steel clad back/regal figure moved gracefully*

her *scream cut through the stillness of the great hall/tears dampened her tunic*

his *people were weighing her in the balance/temper had fair overcome him/thundered commands*

how many men-at-arms will you take

humdudgeon ~ a loud complaint or noise

I *grant you she's comely, but/sorrow at our parting*

I have loved others, Sassenach—but you alone hold all my heart, whole in your hands

I haven't had my woman's flow ~ monthlies

I might that ~ I might

if a child was deformed, or if the father had any other reason not to accept it, the infant would be abandoned to die of exposure

if you captured someone, everything he had on him became yours

in homes of the nobility, gentry, and wealthy townspeople, the birthing room would be freshly-swept and have clean rushes

in medieval London, laws regarding the rights of orphans were careful to place a child with someone who couldn't benefit from his death

in towns, women were usually allowed to do work that involved clothes making, but little else

instincts knelled caution bells

interpreting this as a sign the audience was over

it just be us

kebbie-lebbie ~ a commotion

knight-errant ~ a medieval knight who wandered around looking for *adventure/work*

last eventide

layby

laying his dirk aside

leave the premises posthaste

leaves on the morrow

led to a copse by a stream

let us make haste

life as a servant for the rich was all many women could hope for

like a *loyal shieldmate/lute to a minstrel's touch*

limned

mandrake ~ deadly, but also used as an anesthetic for surgery; used to put a person to sleep

me thinks I judged you too harshly

medical care was poor, so childbirth was dangerous

medieval guilds frequently barred women from joining them

medieval period (the Middle Ages) lasted from the 5th through 15th centuries (500-1500)

memories are long (feuds)

mense ~ household

midwives usually had more than a decade of experience, and would be accompanied by assistants she was training

midwives could perform the rite of baptism if they thought the child would die and there was no man nearby to do it

mind you the

moon's passing ~ one month

most babies were swaddled to help their arms and legs to grow straight

most wives from rich families usually didn't look after their own children; they had wet nurses

mothers-to-be would be attended by midwives

mourning brooch

moving quietly so as not to awaken those sleeping on nearby rushes and benches, she

musk mallow ~ used to treat inflammation

must be balmy to consider it

my patience is sore tested

news of their betrayal had reached the Queen's ears

nighean na galladh [nee-an na Gallag] ~ daughter of a bitch

no the now ~ not now

not until she was fair crashing into ~ almost

oaks, beech, holly, birch and pine trees

often a newborn would be placed before its father; if he picked the child up, it meant the babe would be allowed to live and it would be considered a member of the family

oh, do cease your nattering

old methods to hopefully make you have your baby ~ Castor oil will just give you the runs. Sex is the scientifically proven method as semen contains prostaglandins. Clary sage in your bath or rosemary leaf tea are the herbal methods. Walking, walking, walking. Black and Blue cohosh

older boys wrestled, shot with bow and arrow, and engaged in mock battles with staffs and sticks

one of the greatest knights of the realm

only the vexing man

onward they trod

pah ~ used to show disgust, contempt, or annoyance

papist ~ Catholic

passing furious

peace, my Lady

perforce ~ by or through necessity, necessarily, inevitability

placing a sprig in a baby's cradle would protect the child from faeries

played a game of draughts

poetry babbling knave

poor women not only had to work, they had to watch and care for their children

prideful woman

primroses (in Scotland)

pulling his legs up to his chest to accommodate his tall length ~ tub

quit the hall

quite ~ very

quitting the chamber

removed his dirk and scabbard from his belt

ride with God, the Herald shouted (joust)

running betwixt them

Sacred Tree of Life

saint's bones

saints *preserve/protect* me

Saturday fortnight ~ two weeks from this Saturday

raids were an ever-present danger

send them back from whence they came

sennight ~ one week

several maidens had cast their eyes upon him

she has the second sight

she's *increasing (pregnant)/too headstrong by half*

sheathed the sword in the scabbard at his hip

sheep dotted the fields

showed a lot of courage, lass

Sironi ~ the earth healer; serpent was the ancient symbol

snatched the missive back

so, too ~ also

some marriages were planned while the bride-and groom-to-be were still in the cradle

some women may have given birth in a sitting or squatting position

spear ~ only weapon allowed a squire

stars, woman

stayed closeted in her chamber

steeling herself for the king's verdict

stomped back to his camp, cursing all the way

stone ~ 14 pounds ~ weight

stormed through the Hall like a maddened bull

strong-willed lass prevailed

Suono Stone ~ Pictish ~ in Forres

swept her a mocking bow

take your ease for a while

Talisman ~ stone worn around the neck to ward off evil spirits. Had pictures painted on them

tannasg & tannasgach ~ ghosts & spirits

the *bard's tale/chieftain is powerful/king's demands are not negotiable*

the Church limited the number of godparents to three: a godmother and two godfathers for a son; a godfather and two godmothers for a daughter

the *day bonny and warm/flutter of the standards*

the *foothills of a majestic mountain range/market was a tapestry of colors*

the *image of her coupling with/keys of authority at her waist*

the king's knights numbered at least three times his own—the knight set spurs to his steed and

the kings and nobles, for their part, were not only intelligent and appreciative audiences for gifted skalds; some of them were poets in their own right

the *mind-picture tormented his soul/nasal guard of his helmet*

the *oath I have sworn before you today/people enslaved by the victors*

the tidings of ~ news of

the *Welsh were a reticent, closed-mouthed people/woman has made you weak*

their *first couplings/pennons fluttering proudly*

there is trouble afoot ~ people plotting against you

there was no *help against the king's wrath/one here to challenge a battle-ready warrior*

there's a pity for ye

they *are going to be working hand in glove throughout/quit the room/want a parlay*

think you I would

this *week/sennight* past

thought her a toothsome creature

three/however many moons from now

to melt the enemy's resolve

touched his helmet, and turned his horse toward the sidelines

touchstone ~ good luck stone worn around the neck, had painted pictures on them

travel with but *however many* knights

unbiddable girls were beaten into submission

unfastened his gambeson and poleyns

troublesome wench

turned a baleful eye on

Twelfth night ~ January 5th

unhand her

until he hies himself off, this is no place for a lady

vambrace

varlet ~ a knight's page; a rascal; a knave

vexed him apurpose

vindicating his lady's honor

waited until she was out of sight and then strode into the castle

wanted to share his lady love with his people

warmed the bed of

water kelpie

Waverly Station ~ Edinburgh

we *bring the worst tidings/know not what awaits*

wee lordling

what *dost thou need/has befallen/made him so dangerous was/say you we/was the knave up to*

when her introduction to court goes awry

whence hail you

will even grant you leave to

with a tinkling laugh that carried across the great hall

within a wealthy family producing a male heir was imperative

woe betide anyone who

women *couldn't own any property unless they were widows/not allowed to divorce their husbands*

women expected to obey not only their father, but also their brothers and any other male members of the family

wondered what was afoot

would *be bruised by the morrow/give her the sad tidings soon enough*

would *have him drawn and quartered if he learned of/postpone his departure until the morrow*

ye *complement each other/drive me mad/great fool of a man*

ye'er a rascal

yea, nay

yestermorn

you *are an amazement, eschews/bade me*

you *cannot gammon me/devil's spawn*

you go too far, *my lord (or whoever)*

you will not *do whatever* until I grant you leave

young boys followed their fathers around at work or in the fields

young girls 'helped' their mothers at home with simple chores

B. Scottish

*~

a muckle fuss over

a wall of dark clouds rolled around Dunrobin

an old iron key

ancient Celts celebrated the earthly forces; spirals are a natural force pattern found in wind and water currents; they represent a continuity of life – with no beginning and no end – and the pathway that leads to the divine source

and nocht else ~ nothing else

Andrew de Moray ~ led with William Wallace at the Battle of Stirling Bridge; most historians attribute the battle's strategy to de Moray. He was injured during the battle and only lived a few weeks afterward. He and Wallace were jointly named 'leaders of the army of the realm of Scotland.' Both received their knighthood after the battle as well

are *ye/you addled/mad/cracked*

art better? ~ are you better

as *he and his retainers rode through his lands/if pierced by St. George's sainted blade itself*

as *prickly as a gorse bush to/they rode for the safety of the castle*

at *screech o'day/their posts, guards nodded*

attacked the rushes with renewed vigor

attained the spurs of knighthood

awed by the balance between king and protector, the symbiotic relationship that went back at least a thousand years in their royal traditions

aye, she said to herself

Baliol

Balmoral ~ the Queen's favorite place to catch up with her family; on the River Dee

barely *however many* moons of age

barley for honey mead

Battle of Stirling Bridge

battled straw targets and leather dummies

be *merciful, my lord/ye vexed*

bear up, lass

beastie ~ horse

bedeviled his every waking thought

beeswax candles

befool ~ make a fool of

befouled his plans

beg your leave

began the task of pleating his plaid

begone *from here/I say*

Bel's fires ~ swearing

Ben Nevis, Scotland's highest mountain, looms over the still waters of Loch Linnhe

black pudding ~ blood pudding

blatherskite ~ braggart

bloody daft in the head

bonny bride

Border reivers ~ speed was the key to their success

Bruces and McDougals fought a lot

burn ~ a river, creek, stream (Scotland and Northern England)

but for the nonce I must

but soon or late it will be

by *St. George's sword/the Rood*

can ye not ~ can't you?; you can't?

Carnoustie ~ club since around 1850, but golf had been played there since the 1500s

caught a waft of sweet fragrance from the nearby heather

cease, wench

Celtic ~ almond shaped eyes and slanted cheekbones often proclaim this heritage

Celtic cross

Celtic horse ~ emblem of power and sovereignty

chasing down reivers

cheek by jowl

contentment wrapped around him like a well-worn *plaid*

copper beech trees

Cream of the Well ~ New Year's Day ~ if the man drinks of it after accepting it from the lass' hand, he'll fall in love and marry her within the year. Must drink before sunset on New Year's Day

Culloden ~ used pikes - called push of pikes; pike drill very difficult to coordinate. Musketeers needed protection while they reloaded; that's where the pike came into play; they had to cover while the muskets were being reloaded. Otherwise after shooting the one round, the person could only use the musket as a spear

custom dictated the first part of the marriage vows be spoken outside the chapel

did I not know ~ (if I didn't know)

didst thou?

dinna fash yersel'

dinna get in a kerfuffle

do not be *a daftie/churlish*

do not say me nay

do you *misspeak/want it or no*?

do you not ~ don't you

don't ill wish them. It comes back on you

drifted perilously close to the borderlands

drove him daft with

Elizabeth Bruce ~ maiden name deBurgh; her father Edward deBurgh was the Irish Earl of Ulster

feckless

fell into the bracken and

Ferguson ~ MacFhearghuis

first foot ~ piece of coal; added to the fireplace ~ loaf of bread; place on the table ~ bottle of whisky; pour a drink for everyone ~ do not speak until the first footer has wished everyone a happy new year

first foot toast ~ lang may yer lum reek (long may your chimney smoke ~ or however long you live)

fixed his dirk in the front of his belt

folding the many yards of plaid

Forth Bridge ~ cantilever trusses and diamond shaped towers

from whence *do you hail?/she might have come*

gangly wee lad

gaping at her like some moon calf

garrons ~ Scots ponies

gave no credence to her bletherings

God's *teeth/wounds*

good eventide ~ good-night

gorse and heather on the hills

grant me this boon

Hadrian's Wall ~ built by the Romans to separate England from Scotland. Had a stone turret 20 feet high which was used as a lookout post, symbols of phalluses carved into the stone; they were there to fend off the evil eye (superstition)

handfasted ~ without benefit of clergy for a year and a day; then the couple decides if they want to stay married

handsome, bekilted Scotsman

haste ye back

have *a care, lass/been wont to call me/the right of it*

he's a braw laddie

heather hills

heaven forfend ~ heaven forbid

heaven forfend she would

heed me well, *my lady/wench/milady/woman*

heed my words, wench

his faint burr was thickening from temper

his plaid belted low on his waist and hooded over his head

hope to end the feud before it ends in even more death

hounds teeth ~ swearing

how came you here?

I always knew you were addled

I bade you to be quiet, woman

I can that ~ I can

I disremember who told me

I entreat and beseech you

I give you ~ introducing

I give you welcome

I will have a boon for my silence

I trow ~ I vow

I'll hear none of your blather

icy Highland wind

in a land where the history dates back centuries

in July, at Brechin, Baliol renounced his kingdom to Edward Plantagenet's representative, Anthony Bek, the Bishop of Durham, he placed his staff of office in Bek's hands

in sooth ~ in truth

keep your tongue between your teeth

kilt swirling about his powerful legs

king of Dalraida

King Robert the Bruce

let him have a look, aye

Loch Lomond – supposedly site of one of Arthur's twelve battles

looked every inch the laird of

Lord of Misrule ~ at New Years' festivities

macdacht

make haste if you want to

making inroads with the other chieftains

mere slip of a lass

mist enshrouded hills

mist shrouded *loch/moor*

neatly folded its great length

nostalgic sound of bagpipes

on the morrow

pining for Scotland

pressed his heels to the flank of the garron and rode forward

pressed his heels into the garron's flanks

Ragman Roll ~ listing of names of men who pledged their fealty to Edward Plantagenet and who reconfirmed getting their Scottish lands back after Baliol was deposed

reivers ~ men from another clan who stole cattle

rippling waters of the loch

Robert and Elizabeth Bruce were married for 25 years

Robert Bruce ~ the Earl of Carrick/lived at Lochmaben

Robert Bruce's enemy was Comyn

said in a booming brogue

Sassenach ~ foreigner/Englishman

Scots ale

slashing with the broadsword he held clasped in both hands

snatched for his dirk and lunged for

snorting black destrier

snow covered moors

the Bruce was a champion at wrestling

the buttery ~ a Scottish bread roll; storeroom for liquor

the noo ~ now

to the skirl of pipes

tossing the garron's reins to

trampled the heather beneath their horses' hooves

tumbled head over arse

unbelted and unpinned his plaid, letting it fall to the floor

unbelting his plaid and removing his shirt, he

was a sonsie lass

whisky (with no e)

wi' ~ with

William Wallace ~ bound on a hurdle and dragged behind horses through London, from Westminster to the gallows at Smithfield. He was hoisted with a noose about his neck, but let down while still alive. His genitals were cut off and his bowels were torn out (but still attached) and burned in a fire while he was still alive. He was then beheaded and his body cut into four pieces. His head was spiked on London Bridge; his right leg was sent to Berwick, his left to Perth, his right arm to Newcastle and his left to Stirling

winter in the Highlands ~ exceedingly fierce and cruel ~ very hard to fight in the winter

ye wee bit fool

ye'd better plant no seeds in the laird's furrow

Scottish Words

*~

a bheanachd [a ve-anakd] ~ my blessing

a bhoireanaich ~ woman

a bhràthair ~ brother

a choin ~ dog

a chuisle ~ my heart's blood

a Dhia, cuidich mi [a jee-yah] ~ Oh God, help me

a dheobhhail [a yeavuil] ~ you devil

a ghraidh~ less formal version of mo ghraidh ~ my love

a leannan ~ sweetheart

a mhic an diabhoil [A vihe an dia vail] ~ you son of the devil ~ swearing

a muirninn [a voornin] ~ my darling

aboot ~ about

an e'n fhirinn a th'agad m'annsaachd? [An e'n iirin a h'agad ansakd?] ~ Do you tell me the truth, my love?

ar 'n athair ~ Our Father

arisaid ~ shawl

athair ~ father

bairn ~ child/infant

balach biodheach [Balak bauiak] ~ beautiful boy

ban ~ female

ban-lichtne ~ female healer

beadraich [bet-a-reise] ~ caress

beannachd ~ blessed

beannachd leat ~ goodbye

beannachd leat, a charaid ~ goodbye, old friend

boidheach ~ beautiful

broch ~ tower

buidheachas, mo charaid ~ thank you, friend

cailleach ~ an old woman/divine hag

ceilidh [KAY lee] ~ celebration/party

charaid ~ friend

chirurgeon ~ surgeon

chridhe [cree] ~ heart

ciamar a tha thu [Kia-mar a haa u] ~ How are you?

ciamar a tha tu, mo chridhe? [Kia-mar a haa u, mo crie-e?] ~ How are you, my heart (darling)?

claidheamh mor ~ great sword

creach ~ booty, plunder, prey, quarry/reiving

Dhia ~ God

doun ~ down

droch aite [drok aaite] ~ bad place

eudail [ay-dahl] ~ darling

feasgar math [fesgur mah] ~ good afternoon

feileadh-mor ~ ancient kilt/belted plain kilt

gaolach ~ dear

ghràdhich ~ *love*

ghràdhiche [gah-rAg-heeyah] ~ *lover*

go raith maith agat ~ thank you

gomeral ~ fool

is mise ~ I am

latha math ~ good day

leannan ~ lover, sweetheart, etc.

loch ~ lake

luaidh mo chèile [loy mo heeluh] ~ love of my life

m' annsachd ~ my best beloved

m'fheudail ~ my darling

madainn mhath [mahteen vah] ~ good morning

màthair ~ mother

mellheidit ~ a person who is stupid/dull/oafish

mo anam cara ~ soulmate (soul friend)

mo cáran ~ my love

mo chridhe [mo cree] ~ my heart

mo eudail [ay dahl] ~ my darling

mo ghràidh [mo graag] ~ my love/dear

mo gràdhaiche [mo ga-rag-e heeyuh]~ my lover

*mo leannan [*mo le-anan*]* ~ my sweetheart

mo luaidh [mo luai] ~ my beloved, darling

mo maise [mo vaishe] ~ my beauty

mo nighean [mo nee-an] ~ my girl, my lass

mo ghràidh ~ my love

mòran taing [moran tang] ~ many thanks

muckle ~ large

oidhche mhath [oykah vah] ~ good night

oot ~ out

ruaidh [rooagh] ~ red (i.e. a person's hair, a nickname)

Samhainn ~ October 31st, The Feast of All Hallows

Saorsa [Soor-sa] ~ freedom

se do bheatha [sheh doe VEH-huh] ~ you're welcome

Seanachaide ~ storyteller

Seanachaidh/seneschal ~ storyteller

sgian dubh ~ a small Scots knife

sguir [sgooir] ~ stop

slàinte! ~ cheers

slàinte mhoire ~ good health/cheer

taitinn [tock- schcheen] ~ please

tapadh leat [TAH-puh LAHT] ~ thank you

Tha gaol agam ort ~ I love you

Tha gaol agam oirbh, agus bithidh gu bràth ~ I love you. I always will

Tha mi duilich ~ I'm sorry

thalla le Dia ~ go with God

tioraidh ~ bye

uisge beatha ~ the water of life

C. Irish

*~

'tis a fine and glorious pleasure to make yer acquaintance, me pretty wee lass

'tis a pretty thing, so *it/she* is

'tis all most o' us can ask for, at all

'tis meself, at all

'tis not *whoever* I'm after wanting to see

'tis the way it's always been, to be sure

'twas a grand house, indeed

a cross of rowan wood to get you under the eyes of the wee folk without waking the watchers *a cuishle mo croidh* ~ pulse of my heart

a grand soft day

a harp ~ the symbol of Ireland

a man played a plaintive tune on the fiddle

a member of the Quality

a roaring turf fire blazed in the huge fireplace

a tin whistle piping a sweet lament

ah, would I be after doin' that now, me darlin'

amn't I'm still here

an invitation to stay and have a sup of tea

and in time, please God, our children

and more's the pity, so

and sure, amn't I the best man for the position

and there's an end of it ~ that's all

are ye after offerin' a man a mouthful of tay, then

are you after forgetting

as the old Irish saying goes, I'm going to ask her to hang her laundry next to mine

Ascendancy

began to fooster about with

best you go when the moon is bloat

Blaithin ~ name ~pronounced blaw heen

bless God that ye've

blessed Saint Bridget

blood pounded in his veins like the deep thud of the *bodhran*, the Irish drum that drove a mighty rebel song

blue for good fortune and joy

cack-handed ~ awkward

carrying thyme in her wedding bouquet meant a girl was pure, untouched

Colcannon ~ a dish of mashed potatoes with cabbage and wild scallions

come to spend the Christmas with us

come ye inside

curse the memory of his black soul

don't be worrying

ducked through the low doorway and drew in a lungful of yeast and turf smoke

Eire ~ pronounced air a

eyes huge and gray and long-lashed, they were

fancy a bite at

farl ~ bread ~ any of various quadrant-shaped flatbreads and cakes, traditionally made by cutting a round into four pieces. In Northern Ireland, the term generally refers to soda bread and to potato bread or cakes

footing the jig on a summer's eve

gathered for a bit of a dance

gathered of an evening

God's blessing on you, Mrs. *Whoever*, 'tis a fine day, at all

had been bosom friends since

he did, at all

he'd had his way with her, so he had, kissing her until she was senseless

he's a great age on him

he's become full of bigness, so he has

hedge schools ~ so called because they were held in secret, often in the country, and sometimes behind hedges so they couldn't be seen from the road

her fingers on the harp were light and sure

her whispered words fell on him like the rain on a soft day

hung for a sheep as a lamb

I can help them, so I can

I can't serve ye, and there's an end of it

I will, to be sure

I'd welcome a heat o' the fire, so

I'll put the kettle on the hob

I'm afraid I'm after tellin' a lie to

I'm after having a pint before I make me way home

I'm after having a wee mouthful at *wherever/whatever restaurant*

I'm after needin' a private word with you, my friend

I'm after speaking to him, if you please

I'm away to bed

I've to be at the Big House tomorrow

if 'tis a tale you're after telling me

Irish babies weren't swaddled during the medieval period

is anything up?

is it yerself, *Whoever*

isn't it them that's after paying the rent

jewelry (Claddagh ring) ~ heart toward you means your heart is taken; heart away means your heart is free

Liam ~ Irish name for William ~ Willeen, derogatory term for it

liked nothing better than a bit of a dance

meet the lads at the crossroads dance of a summer evening

merciful Mary!

not alone was she ~ not only

not very well liked ~ not in the times that are in it

o'yourn ~ of yours

oh, aye

oh, but he was a charming one, so he was

oh, Mary Mother of God

one day they'll be after thanking me

open it, do

opened the press

passage on the packet steamer to arrange

played haunting melodies on the harp

played the fiddle, danced and sang the *comallyes*

please God they will

praties were the size of marbles

pull us a pint, will you please

pulled a tin whistle from his pocket and ambled over to

say you understand, do

scrubbed a few clods of mud from his brogues

she'd wanted to run away then, far away from hunger and disease

she's a lovely one, so she is

Sheary ~ Irish for Jeffrey

smoke rose in a lazy plume from his *duideen*, the tiny clay pipe clenched between his teeth

so many lost to hunger and death, fevers, and emigration

so many shades of green he'd lost count

so they *are/were*

so, he's after needing a wife, is he

sung and played the fiddle and the tin whistle and the *bodhran*

sure she's fine

sure that was disappointing

sure, I'm just as able for it

sure, if I refuse you, won't you be after running to himself with the tale

sure, there's

sure, wasn't I after meeting with *whoever*

sure, weren't they afeared o'

sure, you haven't lived until you've had

sweet Mary and St. Patty

sweet *Mother of God/Saint Patrick*

the fine bright colleen

The Ladies' Watch ~ ruined tower over Galway Bay that had witches (drowned Vikings); sent their longboats crashing against the rocks

the potato blight destroying lives

the reek of *whiskey/poitin* was still strong

the rock who'd kept them together when the hunger was at its worst

the sweet smile of her

the tears soaked the coarse wool of his fisherman's sweater

the zing of the fiddle or the plaintive trill of the tin whistle

they know how to entertain, so they do

they saw the snow, so they did, and nothing would do but that they go out to play

they're after sayin' 'tis some

they're saying he's after going over the water, at all, to find work

tiny white cottages dotted the hills, long stone fences separating them

vowed to have nothing to do with the secret societies that marauded about the country, looking for ways to sabotage the landlords—the enemy—and eventually set Ireland free

walked into Mass of a Sunday morning

we knew you'd like that, so we did

wee gossoons playing by the strand

went to *Whoever's* Bar of an evening

weren't ye after getting a few shillings fer that

what is you're after wanting more than anything else in the world

whiskey (with an e)

will I be after pourin' some *tea/coffee/chocolate*

will ye try, me darlin' girl

women wore skirts to their ankles over plain blouses, covered with plaid shawls

would ye come for a ramble with me

ye'll be after *knowin'/meetin'* him, so you will

ye're a sight for sore eyes, lad, so ye are

ye're no longer welcome here, boy-o

ye've brought the good weather with you, so you have

you'll be telling her to

you're hurt, so you are, and

you've been good to me, so you have, and sure, I'll always love you

you've the look of your mother

Irish Words

~

a chroí ~ [uh KHREE] ~ heart

a chuisle, a chroí ~ my pulse, my heart

a chuisle mo chroí ~ [muh khish-la] ~ pulse of my heart

a ghrá ~ [uh GHRAH] ~ love

a mhuirnín ~ [uh WUR-neen] ~ darling

a stór ~ [uh stohr] ~ my treasure

acushla ~ darling

Ádhraím thú ~ I adore you

an bpósfaidh tú mé? ~ will you marry me

an dúidín ~ small clay pipe (duideen)

an gorta mor ~ the great hunger

anamchara ~ soulmate

ath bhliain faoi mhaise ~ Happy New Year

bodhrán ~ Irish drum

boreen ~ country lane or narrow, unpaved road

buíochas ~ thanks

buíochas le Dia ~ thank God!

cairde ~ friend

coinneal mór na Nollaig ~ the great Christmas candle, still burned in the window (lasted one week) (According to tradition, the candle served as a symbol of welcome to Mary and Joseph who sought shelter on that first Christmas Eve)

comallyes ~ ancient Irish songs, ballads

craic ~ celebration/fun/entertainment

cronaím thú ~ I miss you

culchie ~ someone from outside Dublin; rural Ireland

dea-tráthnóna mo bhean álainn ~ good evening my lovely wife

duideen ~ tiny clay pipe

dullahan (Gan Ceann) ~ the fairy horseman without a head

dúmhál ~ blackmail

fáinne ~ ring

fíorghrá ~ true love

flaithuil

go deo na ndeor ~ forever

go raibh maith agat ~ thank you

go síoraí ~ forever

grá go deo ~ forever love

grá mo chroí ~ love of my heart

Is breá liom tú ~ I love you; like you a lot

Is tú mo ghrá ~ I love you

le grá go deo ~ with love forever

m'fhíorghrá ~ [MEER-ggrah] ~ my true love

machushla ~ darling; a special loved one

míle buíochas ~ a thousand thanks/many thanks

mo áilleacht ~ my beauty

mo chroí ~ my heart

mo éan beag ~ my little bird

mo féileacán ~ my butterfly

mo ghrá amháin ~ my only love

mo gráh ~ my love

mo lasair álainn ~ my beautiful flame

mo mhíle stór ~ my dearest

mo nighean donn [mo nee-an down] ~ my brown haired lass

mo nighean dubh [mo nee-an dooh] ~ my dark one

mo shíorghrá ~ [muh HEER-ggrah] ~ my eternal love

na mban ag breathnú, the Ladies' Watch. The ruined tower looked out over Galway Bay. 'Twas said a coven of witches once climbed up to the battlements to scour the sea for invaders. According to legend, their spells whipped up a fierce storm that sent a fleet of Viking longboats crashing against the rocks. All but a handful of Vikings perished, and those that survived came ashore and were enslaved by the witch women

póg ~ kiss
póg mo thóin! [po-og mo ho-on] ~ kiss my ass!
poitín ~ whiskey
seanchaidhe ~ storyteller
sionnach [Shionak] ~ fox
síorghrá ~ eternal love
slán agat ~ goodbe for now (said by the person leaving)
slán leat ~ goodbye for now (said by the person remaining)
tá tú go h-álainn ~ you're beautiful
táim i ngrá leat ~ I'm in love with you
the Dullahan ~ the fairy horseman without a head
Tuatha Dé Danann of Irish mythology
Uigingeach ~ Irish for Norseman

D. Additional Extras ~ Both Scottish and Irish

~

a candle in the window ~ to guide the stranger on Christmas Eve
amadán ~ a fool
athair [AH her] ~ father
Céad Míle Fáilte! ~ one hundred thousand welcomes
comforting, like the soft patter of rain on thatch
drew a cup of heather ale
jerked her attention from the simmering turf fire to *whoever*'s penetrating gaze
là breith sona dhuit ~ Happy Birthday to you
máthair [MAW her] ~ mother
mist veiled the moor
mists encircling him
nor ~ then (someone better nor me)
several fishing boats made their way across
suffered much beneath the heel of the English

the deep thud of the *bodhran* ~ drum

the saints preserve him

white pudding ~ oat and fat sausage often eaten at breakfast, common in Ireland and Scotland

Add Your Own Medieval Tags!

~

3

CHRISTMAS

~

(*nolek aheeyarakhugus bleeana yahoor*)

a holiday *dream comes true/full of miracles*

a warm holiday glow

according to *A Celebration and History* (ISBN 0-679-74038-4), by Leigh Grant, the written lyrics to 'The Twelve Days of Christmas' first appeared in *Mirth without Mischief* in the early 1780s in England. Grant states that the tune to which these words are sung apparently dates back much further and came from France. *Mirth without Mischief* describes 'The Twelve Days of Christmas' as a type of memory game played by children. A leader recited the first verse, the next child recited the second verse, and so on until someone missed a verse and had to pay some kind of penalty in the game

adds to the holiday elegance

Advent is solemn and religious in spirit

ancient Scandinavia and the Norse mythology is where the tale of kissing under the mistletoe came into being

annual Christmas gala

another possible theory about 'The Twelve Days of Christmas' ~ during the period 1558 to 1829 Catholics in England were prohibited from any practice of their faith by law—private or public. It was a crime to be a Catholic. Some people say the song was written to help young Catholics learn the tenets of their faith during that period when to be caught with anything in 'writing' indicating adherence to the Catholic faith could not only get you imprisoned, but could also get you hanged, drawn and quartered. The song's gifts are allegedly hidden meanings to the teachings of the faith. 'True Love' refers to God. 'Me' refers to Christians. Other hidden meanings in the verses are:

- 'partridge in a pear tree' ~ Jesus Christ who died on a tree as a gift from God

- 'two turtle doves' ~ Old and New Testaments - another gift from God
- 'three French hens' ~ faith, hope and love - the three gifts of the Spirit that abide (I Corinthians 13)
- 'four calling birds' ~ four Gospels which sing the song of salvation through Jesus Christ
- 'ive golden rings' ~ first five books of the Bible also called the 'Books of Moses'
- 'six geese a-laying' ~ six days of creation
- 'seven swans a swimming' ~ seven gifts of the Holy Spirit (I Corinthians 12:8-11; Romans 12, Ephesians 4; I Peter 4:10-11)
- 'eight maids a milking' ~ eight beatitudes
- 'nine ladies dancing' ~ nine fruits of the Holy Spirit (Galatians 5:22 & 23)
- 'ten lords a-leaping' ~ Ten Commandments
- 'eleven pipers piping' ~ eleven faithful disciples
- 'twelve drummers drumming' ~ twelve points of the Apostles' Creed

around Victorian times a traditional Christmas feast was roasted goose or roasted turkey. Most Londoners would have been familiar with the 'goose club', which was a method of saving to buy a goose for Christmas. Goose clubs were popular with working-class Londoners, who paid a few pence a week toward the purchase of a Christmas goose. The week before Christmas, London meat markets were crammed with geese and turkeys, many imported from Germany and France, although some were raised in Norfolk, and taken to market in London. The birds were walked from Norfolk to the markets in London; to protect their feet the turkeys had 'boots' made of sacking or leather and geese had their feet protected with a covering of tar

bustling Christmas cheer

by the 18th century in Britain, it became popular to create a ball of mistletoe that would be hung as a Christmas decoration. If a couple was found standing under the mistletoe, they were then obliged to kiss if the mistletoe ball still had berries. For each kiss, one berry would be taken from the ball. Once all the berries were gone, all the 'luck' in love and marriage was considered to be drained out of the mistletoe and it was now considered bad luck to kiss beneath it, instead of good luck as before

crib ~ nativity scene/*crèche*

Christ's Mass ~ Christmas

Christmas greenery

Christmas Pudding ~ everyone in the household must take turns stirring the pudding and make a wish; the mixture should be stirred from east to west, in honour of the three wise men

clusters of mistletoe

cracker ~ small parcel that makes an explosive report when pulled from both ends, traditionally pulled at Christmas

during the ancient 12-day Christmas celebration, it was considered unlucky to let the log in the fireplace stop burning. This log was called the Yule log and would be used to light the fire in the New Year, to ensure that good luck carried on from year to year. The Yule Log custom was handed down from the Druids

European mistletoe often grows on apple trees; more rarely on oaks

historically, mistletoe represents romance, fertility, and vitality

holiday trimmings

I think we're going to need a miracle. Well 'tis the season for it

in Scandinavia, mistletoe was considered a plant of peace, under which enemies could declare a truce or warring spouses kiss and make-up. Eighteenth-century English were credited with a certain magical appeal called a kissing ball. At Christmas time a young lady standing under a ball of mistletoe, brightly trimmed with evergreens, ribbons, and ornaments, could not refuse to be kissed. Such a kiss could mean deep romance or lasting friendship and goodwill. If a girl remained unkissed, she could not expect to marry the following year

it was a Christmas Eve long remembered

kisses politely stolen (under mistletoe)

marked the beginning of the holiday

mistletoe ~ often regarded as an aphrodisiac and fertility herb

Mistletoe became associated with Christmas from the tradition of hanging mistletoe in one's home to bring good luck and peace to those within the house. The mistletoe would be hung around the New Year and the previous year's mistletoe would be taken down, with its powers apparently tapped. The new plant would then provide luck throughout the year

Nollaid Aighearach agus Bliadhna Mhath U ~Merry Christmas and Happy New Year

Nollaid Chridheil Huibb ~ Merry Christmas

Saint Steven's Day marks the beginning of the twelve days of Christmas, a light hearted time given over to merry making and fun. It is a holiday of heart-warming homecoming and family gatherings, with candles glowing in the windows as a sign of welcome

small candles on trees

the Christmas Octave ~ begins December 25th

the familiar pages of her Bible

The Feast of the Seven Fishes ~ part of the Italian-American Christmas Eve celebration. Today, it is a feast that typically consists of seven different seafood dishes. It originates, however, from Southern Italy, where it is known as The Vigil (La Vigilia). This celebration commemorates the wait, the *Vigilia di Natale*, for the midnight birth of the baby Jesus

the jingle of the harness

the plant was given the name 'misteltan' in Old English

the simple magic of Christmas

there is a proper etiquette for kissing under the mistletoe: first, the man may only kiss a woman on the cheek and second, when he does so, he removes one berry from the mistletoe sprig. After all the berries are gone, the kissing ends

toll the Devil's knell ~ Christmas

took no notice of the tradition that decorations must wait until Christmas Eve

tree decorations ~ candles adorned the tree; walnuts, orange slices

Victorian sugarplums ~ Christmas

walk-in size hearths were centered on either side of the long walls, decorated with pine garlands and sprigs of holly. Scores of guests sat at mahogany tables, glistening with china and silver

you're the present 'neath my Christmas tree

BONUS EXTRAS ~ TAGS FROM THIS POINT ON CAN BE USED FOR ANY ERA

4

LAUGHING ~ SMILING ~ CRYING

A. Laughing

~

bitterly / confidently / darkly / delightedly /gaily / good-naturedly / grimly / merrily / mirthlessly / sourly

a full rich *chuckle/sound*

a ribald jolt of laughter

a ripple of laughter came from her throat

a rumble of masculine laughter ensued

a soft ripple of laughter escaped her lips

a titter of feminine laughter

added with a *cold laugh/deep chuckle/laugh/thick sneer/wicked grin/wistful sigh*

allowed a *confused/nervous* laugh

almost *chortled/giggled at his actions*

an *easy laugh escaped her/evening filled with laughter*

an exasperated laugh sounded quietly on his lips

another brittle, bitter laugh

answered, laughing

barely suppressed laughter *erupted/spread*

barked *a derisive laugh/out a laugh that wasn't far from hysteria*

began laughing again

bitter laughter

boisterous laughter

boyish giggles

broke *into gales of unrestrained laughter/off suddenly in laughter*

broke out in rich, hearty laughter

burst out laughing

choked *back another chortle/on a bark of bitter laughter*

choking on a laugh

chortled with glee

chuckled *and drew her toward him/at her sour expression*

chuckled *softly/with her*

chuckled, a fond look on his face

clamor of conversation and laughter

clamping her lips together she repressed a sudden laugh

could hear the laughter and the booming voices of men

could no longer contain his laughter

couldn't keep back the chuckle that bubbled in his throat

couldn't suppress the laughter that erupted

covered her mouth to stifle *a/her laugh/laughter*

crowed/cooed/giggled with delight

deep, rich laughter floated up from his throat

delighted, she laughed

despite herself she had to laugh

didn't like the sound of his laughter

doubled over laughing

drunken laughter

enduring his laughter

felt *him shake with silent laughter/his silent chuckle as he held her*

fighting back laughter

filled with the sound of talking and laughing

forced a rusty laugh from his throat

forcing a *laugh/smile*, she

fought against the laughter rising in her throat

gave a bark of *angry/bitter* laughter

gave a *bark/bitter bark* of laughter

gave a *breathless/low/nervous/startled* laugh

gave a dispirited laugh

gave a *hard laugh and turned away/harsh bark of laughter*

gave a *humorless/low* laugh

gave a low, *wicked laugh/mirthless chuckle*

gave a *rumbling/small/soft/startled* laugh

gave a short, *despairing/humorless* laugh

gave a shrill laugh

gave a *small, defeated laugh/snort of laughter*

gave in to laughter again

genuine laughter as free of derision as a child's

giddy with laughter

had a hysterical urge to laugh

hadn't laughed so much in years

half laugh, half sob

hard-pressed not to break out laughing

harsh *and jarring laughter followed his words/laughter broke from him*

he couldn't suppress a chuckle

he gave a deep, rumbling laugh

he laughed again, but this time there was an edge to it

he laughed, *but it sounded forced to her/further unnerving her*

he laughed, not a guffaw, but a robust belly laugh

he laughed, sending her a mischievous wink

he scarcely refrained from laughing out loud

heard the bark of his laughter

hearing her carefree laughter

her *giggle/good humor* was contagious
her laughter bubbled up
her *little girl/throaty* laughter filled the room
her uncertain laugh
his *answering laughter rang deep and rich/bitter laugh*
his chest shook with suppressed laughter
his deep chuckle sounded
his deep, booming laugh echoed through the room
his harsh laugh sounded more like a sob
his *jeering laughter/laugh held no humor*
his laugh *was mocking/mocked her*
his laughter was *harsh and bitter/without amusement*
his massive shoulders shook with laughter
his return laughter caught her by surprise
his throaty laughter filled the air
his/her ready laugh
hollow laughter
humiliated among roars of laughter and jeers
humorless, bitter laugh
husky timbre of his laugh
ignored her snort of laughter
in spite of herself she laughed
interrupted with a deep laugh
jovial laughter filled the air
joyous laughter bubbled up in her chest and burst forth
laugh *deep and warm/drifted on the wind*
laugh gave away how really tired she was
laughed *a lot at the gentlemen's sallies/aloud at*
laughed *and shook his head/at her in spite of himself*
laughed at *her vehemence/his honesty*

laughed *cooly as/despite herself/in relief/in response/in spite of herself/to herself*

laughed softly, the sound hollow and bitter

laughed then, even though it hurt

laughed without *humor/mirth*

laughed, *a throaty sound/and he chuckled*

laughed, *but it sounded pinched, unnatural/clearly pleased*

laughed. She knew him far too well

laughing *eyes/in delight/with embarrassment*

laughing so hard she could barely breathe

laughter a deep, hearty sound

laughter *boomed/echoed*

laughter *bubbled in her throat/danced in his eyes/deep and throaty/ filled the room/followed him all the way to/in his voice/rang through the hall/rose in his/spilled into*

laughter floated on the soft evening breeze

laughter like the trails of yesterday's tears

laughter *pealed from tables where/rumbled deep in his chest*

let out a bitter laugh

making a poor attempt to control his laughter

nearly laughed aloud, but suppressed the urge

nervous/raucous/teasing/throaty laughter

overjoyed, she was laughing and crying at the same time

put a hand over her mouth to stifle her laughter

remember the rich tenor of his laughter

rewarded with a laugh

she *beamed/bit back a laugh*

she laughed even harder

she laughed, *a light musical sound/but only to hide her pain*

she made a sound, something between a laugh and a sob

she *squealed and giggled/giggled in delight*

short barking laugh

shoulders shook with *mirth/suppressed laughter*

slapping his thigh

slow, nervous laugh slipped through his lips

smothered a laugh with a cough

snatches of laughter

snorted *a laugh in response/an unamused laugh*

spewed the coffee from his mouth, choking on laughter

statement produced more loud guffaws

stifled a *chuckle behind a cough/cry of pain/laugh/startled laugh*

stifled *his/her laughter/tears*

still laughing when

suppressed *a snort of laughter/the laugh waiting to pop out*

the answering peal of laughter

the deep, husky sound of his laughter filled the room

the edges of his lips twitching with suppressed laughter

the rumble of laughter deep in his chest

the sound *a warm rumble/of her laughter*

the sound of his laughter followed her down the hall

the woman had the audacity to laugh in his face

threw back his head and laughed in pure joy

threw back his head and *laughed/barked with laughter/roared with laughter*

threw *back his head with a hearty laugh/his head back in laughter*

tipped his hat and grinned at

tossed her dark curls, smiling

trying hard to look stern while trying not to laugh

turned his head so his grin wouldn't be seen

vented a short, derisive laugh

voiced her protest through joyous laughter, trying and failing to sound stern

when the laughter died she asked about

why had she never laughed or smiled at him that way
with a carefree laugh
with a loud guffaw he
with a rumbling laugh he
with a shout and a laugh
with forced laughter
with his infectious laugh

B. Smiling

~

admiring /affectionate / angry / answering / apologetic / appealing / beaming / beautiful / begrudging / bitter / bitterly / blinding / boyish / brief / bright / brightly / brilliant / broad / broadly / calculating / carefree / carelessly / charming / chilliest / chilly / cold / coldly / comforting / condescending / confident / courageous / crooked / cruel / curt /cynical / derisive / devilish / died / dimmed / disarming / dotingly / dreamy / drowsy / dying / easy / eggagerated / encouraging / engagingly / enigmatic / expectant / faded / faint / faintly/ fake / flashed / fleeting / flickered / forced / gap-toothed / gentle / genuine / good-humored / gratefully / grew / grim / grimly / guiltily / happy / hard / hearty / hesitant / humorless / humorlessly / impishly indulgently / infectious / ingenuously/ kind / kindly / knowing / knowing / knowing / knowingly / lazy / lazily / lopsided / mischievous / mockingly / mysterious / nervous / nervously / open / partial / patiently / persistant / played / playing / proudly / radiant / raffishly /ready / reassuring / reassuringly / reluctant / reproved / rumbling / sadly / sardonic / satisfied / secret / self-mocking / serene / sexy / sheepish / sheepishly / shy / shyly / sleepily / slight / slightly / slow / slowly / small / smug / smugly / soft / sorrowful / startled / stiff / strained / sweetly / sympathetic taunting / tenderly / tentative / tentatively / thin / thinly/ tight / tired / tiredly / trembling / tolerant / toothy / tremulous / triumphant / tugged / tugging / unabashedly /uncertain / uncertainly / understanding / unnerving / unrepentantly /

valiantly / vanished / victorious / wan / wanly / warm / warmly / wary / weak / weary / wicked / wickedly / widening / winning / wistful / wistfully / wobbly / wolfish / wolfishly / wry / wryly

a *begrudging/bright* smile *lit her face/tugged the corner of his mouth*

a *confident/drowsy* smile played *about his mouth/at her lips*

a faint smile curved her *lips/mouth*

a faint smile played *around/over* his *lips/mouth*

a grin split his face

a grin *tugged/tugging* at his mouth

a hard, angry smile played about his mouth

a humorless smile twisted his lips

a knowing smile

a lazy smile *curved his sensual lips/lit his face*

a lazy, *crooked grin/enigmatic half-smile*

a poignant smile *played about the corner of her mouth/curved her mouth*

a proud smile broke across his face

a sad, reminiscent smile played about her lips

a *self-mocking smile touched his lips/silly satisfied grin on his face*

a slight smile *curved/tipped the corners of* his mouth

a slow grin *curving his mouth/spread across his lips*

a slow, *infectious grin spread across his face/secretive smile spread across*

a small smile *playing about his lips/tugged at the corner of his mouth/tugged slowly at her lips*

a smile *curled her pursed lips/lifted the corners of her lips/played around the corners of her mouth*

a smile *played/playing* on *his/her* lips

a smile *pulled at his mouth/slowly curved her lips*

a smile spread about her *face/mouth*

a smile *spread over his lips/stole through*

a smile *tipped/tipping* up *the/one* corner of his mouth

a smile *toyed at one corner of his mouth/tugged at her lips/wreathing his ruddy cheeks*

a smug smile lifted the corner of his mouth

a soft reassuring smile

a tender smile softened his grave expression

a tiny smile tipped the corners of her generous mouth

a weak smile *tugged/tugging* at *his/her lips/mouth*

a wobbly smile touched her lips

a wry *expression crossed his face/smile tipping her lips*

a wry grin *tugged at one corner of his mouth/twitched at his mouth*

a wry half smile that curved his lips

a wry smile *pulled at/twisted* his lips

acknowledged and smiled

allowed *a partial smile/the hint of a smile as*

an *exaggerated/unnerving* smile touched her lips

answered his smile with one of her own

apologetic smile didn't reach his *whatever color* eyes

attempted a smile, but her lips wouldn't cooperate

attempted a smile. It failed to reach her troubled eyes

awoke with a smile on her face

beamed an approving smile

braved a smile *he/she* didn't feel

brought a smile to her lips

cast a warm smile in the young woman's direction

cast his old friend a mysterious smile

checked a smile

chuckled *softly/warmly*

could hear the smile in his voice

couldn't help *but smile/smiling to himself*

couldn't keep the smile from curving his lips

couldn't stop *laughing/smiling*

couldn't stop the grin that curved *his/her* lips

couldn't stop the satisfied smile from curving *his/her* mouth

cruel mouth curved into a smile

face brightened and *he/she* smiled

face devoid of his usual smile

face lit up with a smile

felt *a bubble of laughter rising in his chest/his lips curve into a smile*

flashed a *half-embarrassed/playful/wicked* smile at

flashed *her/them* a *crooked/sheepish* smile

flashed him *a warm, beautiful/her most blinding* smile

for the first time he allowed the hint of a smile

forced a smile while inwardly she winced at the pain

forced a *tired/wobbly* smile

forced *another stiff/herself to* smile

forcing a smile, she

fought to control the smile that tugged at the corners of his mouth

found herself smiling

full lips curving into a smile

full-fledged grin

gave a *comforting/disarming/sympathetic* smile

gave a *startled laugh/toothy grin/weak smile*

gave an *apologetic/encouraging* smile

gave her a disarming smile, then turned and left

gave her a hint of a smile, his lips barely curling upward

gave her a knowing *look/smile*

gave her *a slow, wolfish grin/an almost boyish smile*

gave her *an odd half /his most appealing/no answering* smile gave her what he hoped was a charming smile

gave him a ghost of a smile

gave him a *knowing/nervous/radiant/strained/uncertain/wistful* smile

gave him *a slow, shy/her most charming* smile

gave in gracefully with a smile

gazed at her with a small smile

gentle *face creased in a smile/smile on her face*

gifted him with a blinding smile and blinked innocently

giving him a *knowing/tight/warm* smile

graced her with a *lazy grin/slow smile*

gracing him with a warm smile, she

greeted him with a tight smile and an appraising look

grin *came easily/disappeared and was replaced with a scowl/fell away*

grin faded, but a spark of mischief twinkled in his eyes.

grin slowly faded and heat infused his eyes

grin *splitting his weathered face/stretched from ear to ear/ took up her whole face/tugged at his lips*

grin tugged at the corner of *his/her* lips

grin *turned wry/widening*

grin was *boyishly proud/cold and cruel*

grinned *a lopsided grin/as he helped her to her feet/broadly/from ear to ear/down at her/good naturedly/in spite of himself/in triumph/wide at*

grinned and there was a twinkle to his eyes

grinned at his friend in his lazy, good-natured way

grinned, *glancing at/mocking her with his eyes/pleased/ showing off dimples*

grinning *broadly at/from ear to ear/like a witless fool*

had a slow, easy, confident smile

he smiled, a warm, open smile

heard a smile in his voice
her blinding smile
her own smile died on her lips
her smile *slowly faded/stole his breath away/touched his soul*
hiding a smile behind *his/her* hand
his ready smile vanished when she flung open the door. "What's wrong?"
his sheepish grin speaking for him
his slow smile flashed in the moonlight
his smile doesn't warm his *dark/whatever color* eyes
his smile took the sting from his words
his smile was *cynical/fleeting*
his smug look of satisfaction served to aggravate her further
if a mere smile could turn her knees to little more than melted wax
just looking at her made him smile
labored to give her a smile
lazy smile took her breath away
left *him/her* with one last smile
lips *a tight unsmiling line/curled into a sardonic smile*
lips curved *in a secret smile/in a wide gap-tooth smile/lifted into a lazy smile*
lips *quirked/quivered* with repressed mirth
lips *spread in/tilted in the beginnings of* a smile
lips twisted *in a halfhearted smile/with ill-concealed amusement*
lips twitched *in/with* a humorless smile
lips twitched *upward/with a smile*
looked at him with a shy smile
lovely smile faded
lowered his head, hiding a smile
made her bite back a smile
made no effort to *contain/curb* his smile

managed a *grim/weak* smile

managed to smile for him

managed/manages a wan smile

masked her agitation with a smile

merely nodded and smiled in her direction

met him with a brittle smile

mouth came up in his familiar teasing smile

mouth twisted with *a wry smile/suppressed laughter*

murmured with a wicked smile

near smile surprised and pleased her

nearly made him smile

nodded and smiled

offered a *chilly/comforting* smile/*sheepish half-smile*

offered/offering an apologetic smile

offered/offering him a *reassuring/tentative/tremulous* smile

only just managing a smile as he

pasted on her best fake smile

pasting on what she hoped was a smile, she

peered up at him with a tentative smile

rallied with a weak smile

refrained from smiling

remarked with a wicked smile

replied with a beaming smile

repressed *another/the urge to* smile

returned *his/her/the* smile in *good/full* measure

said with a *chuckle/grin/laugh/deep chuckle/touch of a condescending smile*

said with a *forced/gentle/reluctant/satisfied/shy/slow/trembling/ smug/tolerant* smile

said without a trace of a smile

seeing the *mischief/torment* behind his smile

sent him a *mischievous/serene and enigmatic* smile

shared a smile

she attempted a smile, not quite sure she made it

she *forced a smile to her stiff lips/tried to smile*

she grinned, obviously enjoying every minute of his discomfort

she smiled, *hoping to soften her refusal/though it lasted only a moment*

shot him a *wary/winning* smile

sighed and *his/her* smile fell away

slow *grin/smile teased/twisted* his lips

slow, crooked devilish grin stretched his mouth

slow, *secret/sexy* smile curved his lips

slowly the side of his mouth lifted in a crooked smile

small *knowing smile curved his/reproving smile*

smile *barely lifted his lips/broadened to a grin*

smile *broke over his face/crept across his lips/faded from his face*

smile *curled around her mouth/filled her eyes*

smile didn't *falter/hide the heat in her eyes*

smile disappeared just as quickly as it had arrived

smile faded as he seemed to grasp for the right words

smile falling from *his/her* lips

smile *felt sad and small/filled with affection/filled with unutterable sorrow*

smile *flashed/flickered* on *his/her* face

smile gradually lifted the corners of his mouth

smile lifted *his/her* weathered face

smile lit his handsome features

smile *lit/lights* up her face

smile made *his/her* heart race

smile never failed to warm *him/her*

smile overtaken by the sadness in *his/her* eyes

smile *played/playing about/across his/her* lips

smile polite, but guarded

smile radiated warmth

smile so *beguiling as to rob him of his breath/trusting*

smile started in her heart and worked its way to her face

smile stopped short of *his/her* eyes

smile *stretched wide/that wrapped from ear to ear*

smile teasing the corner of *his/her* lips

smile that hid a keen, intelligent mind and a slightly wicked humor

smile *tinged with sorrow/touched his lips/tugged at the corner of/tugged at his mouth*

smile warmed *him/her* from head to toe

smile was a sexy twist of his lips

smile was as cold as *his/her* heart

smile was *bitter/brief/disarming/hesitant/tired /weary*

smile was *like a gentle caress/so warm/sympathetic/tinged with sadness*

smile wavered as her vision blurred

smiled a cold, calculating smile

smiled *a lopsided grin/admiringly at*

smiled and dipped *his/her* chin

smiled and shook her head graciously

smiled as *he watched the children play/the introductions were made*

smiled at him through *her/fresh* tears of joy

smiled at him, *and then he kissed her/knowing her smile didn't reach her eyes*

smiled at *him/her* before *he/she* left

smiled at his own besotted response

smiled at his taunting comments

smiled at *his/her broadly/happily/persistence/winningly*

smiled at *the thought/their antics*

smiled expectantly, holding out his hand to her
smiled for the first time in days
smiled *his/her* chilliest smile at
smiled in smug assurance
smiled in spite of *himself/herself*
smiled kindly upon her
smiled through *her tears/teary eyes*
smiled to herself as if she knew some secret
smiled to put her at ease
smiled while she screamed and struggled
smiled with *satisfaction/understanding*
smiled without humor
smiled, a cruel twist to his lips
smiled, but the sadness in his eyes remained
smiled, kindness in his eyes
smiling and shaking his head
smiling at *her affectionately/what he saw*
smiling *down into her eyes/eager face/in satisfaction*
smiling for the first time in a long time
smiling *grimly/shyly/tenderly at/through her tears/wistfully at*
smiling with an expression that was far too self-satisfied
smothered a smile behind his hand
soft smile lifted her lips
sorrowful smile answered her questions
stood *and gave him a curt smile/smiling to himself*
strode unsmiling from view
struggled to hide a smile
studying him with a good-humored smile
summoned a *reassuring smile/smile as her breathing returned to normal*
suppressed *a/the* smile that tried to raise *his/her* lips

suppressing a smug grin, he

swallowed *her disappointment and tried to smile/the smile that*

taunting smile

the awareness that bolted through him when she smiled

the barest trace of a smile forming on his lips

the corner(s) of *his/her* mouth *twitched/tightening*

the corners of her *eyes crinkled/mouth seemed to lift in a curious absent smile*

the corners of his *lips/mouth formed/turned* into a crooked smile

the corners of his mouth twitched

the saddest of smiles

the smile *in his eyes/on her face died as*

the tiniest of smiles formed at the corners of his mouth

their faces wreathed in smiles

then his smile faded

tried *not to smile/to keep the smile out of his voice*

tried to smile, but she wasn't very successful

tried to smile. The effort failed

tried to summon a smile

trying not to *grin/smile*

turned to flash him a victorious smile

turned to him with a *brilliant/knowing/tremulous* smile

wanted to slap his smiling face

warm smile put her immediately at ease

was almost smiling

watching her with a soft smile on his face

welcome smile

when an impish smile

when he spotted her, his face lit up with a smile

white teeth shone in a teasing smile

with a *gentle/joyful/slow/weak* smile *he/she*

with a smile *he leaned forward/meant only for him*
with an *impish yet earnest grin/inviting smile*
withheld a smile
words elicited a smile from
wore a mocking smile

C. Crying

~

a harsh sob caught in her throat
a litany of helpless sobs
a quiet sob slipped from her throat
a series of small sobs caught in her throat
a single tear slipped from the corner of her eye
a sob racked her *tender/slender* frame
a sob rose from deep in her chest
a sob welled *in her chest/up inside of her*
a tear trickled down her cheek
agonized sobs
allowed the tears to fall
already he could feel tears welling in her eyes
at last her *sobbing subsided/weeping abated*
barely able to speak through the sobs that shook her wraith-like body
barely suppressed a cry
battled tears
began to sob *silently/quietly*
began to sob. He moved to comfort her
bit down a sob
bit her lip to stifle a cry
blinded by tears
blinked *away tears/back sudden tears/back tears/uncertainly*

blinked back the *foolish/string of* tears that threatened to overcome her

blinked back the tears and put him out of her mind

blinked hard, but the tears broke free anyway

blinked rapidly at the well of tears that threatened to spill over

blinking away tears

body heaving with each giant sob

body shook with silent sobs

bowed her head and started to cry

bowing her head, she sobbed brokenly

breast heaved on a sob

breath caught on a broken sob

breaths came in quick spurts between quiet sobs

brought her shaking hand to her mouth to stifle a sob

brushed away a tear

burst into *a storm of tears/tears and ran*

cast a compassionate glance at her tear-stained face

caught back a sob

choked *back a sob/on her tears*

choked back the tears that threatened

choked pitifully on a heaving sob

choking *back tears, she/on her sobs*

choking up, she

clamped a hand over her mouth to stifle a sob

closed her eyes and felt the moisture *of/from* tears forming behind her eyes

closed her eyes in a vain attempt to stay her tears

closing her eyes against the tears that were coming faster now

closing herself inside the bedroom until she was exhausted from crying

clutched her knees to her chest and began to sob

could *barely see him through her tears/see she was trying hard not to cry*

couldn't abide weepy women

couldn't help it. She burst into a fresh flood of tears

covered her face with her hands and sobbed

cried *into his chest/less easily*

cried out, unable to hide her anguish

cry was agonized

crying *changed nothing/in a crumpled heap on the floor*

crying *pitifully/with relief*

crying would avail her nothing

dabbed at a single tear before it could make its way down her cheek

dabbed at *her/the* tears in her eyes

dabbing *at his eyes/away her tears*

dashed away a traitorous tear

dashing a tear away

dissolved *in tears/into wrenching sobs*

dropped her head and sobbed

each giant sob

evidence of tears

eyes began to sting with hot, unfallen tears

eyes *red and swollen from crying/were red with unspilled tears*

face bent over her arms, weeping into them

face wet with tears

fearing tears would choke her

fell against him, sobbing with utter despair

felt *a sob strangling in her throat/the sting of tears in her eyes*

fighting against tears of panic and despair

fighting back *an onslaught of emotions/fresh tears*

fighting back *her tears and sniffling/the hot sting of tears* fighting the tears that stung the back of her throat

fisted away a tear

fled the room, blinded by tears

flew into his embrace, shaking with silent sobs

fought back *a fresh rush of tears/tears of terror and frustration*

fought the tears that threatened

fresh tears *came, but she blinked them back/spilling from*

fresh tears rolled from her eyes onto cheeks already streaked where tears had fallen and dried

frustrated and close to tears

gave a *cry of astounded shock/keening wail*

gave into her tears

gave way to *a torrent of/the tormented* sobs

great sobs racking her slim body

he could handle almost anything but a woman's tears

he heard the tears in her voice and reluctantly raised his gaze to meet hers

head in hands, she let the tears come

heart-stricken, his own eyes brimming with tears

heavy sobs of despair

held her until her sobs died down

helpless to stem the flow of bitter tears that coursed down her face,

her body shook, racked by sobs

her face *streaked/wet* with tears, desolation sweeping over her

her *long lashes spiked with tears/silent tears ran dry*

her sobs echoing through the mist-shrouded air

her *sobs made further speech impossible/tears came fast and hard*

her strangled sob reverberated in his ears

her tears *depleted, she/spent for a time*

her throat aching, she squeezed her eyes shut against a stinging flood of tears her *throat tight with unshed/vision blurred by inexplicable tears*

her voice *a mix of rage and tears/broke into a sob*

her voice carried an undercurrent of bitterness

her voice caught on a sob, and she flung her arms about his neck

her voice *cracked as emotion takes over/dissolved into tears*

her voice faltered and stopped on a sob

her voice wavered, broke

her words *barely finding voice/caught on a sob/dissolved into a storm of tears*

her wrenching cry froze him in his tracks

holding her breath, trying not to move, not to cry

hoped he couldn't see the tears in her eyes

hot tears *came unbidden to her eyes/filled her eyes*

hot tears *formed behind her eyelids/of anger filled her eyes*

hung her head, staving off the sobs

hysterical tears rose to her eyes

if only tears were laughter

in a flood of tears, she threw herself down on the bed

jammed a fist against her mouth to muffle her sobs

just about to cry when he took her in his arms

kindly lifted her tear-stricken face

laid her head on his chest and sobbed uncontrollably

large *brown/whatever color* eyes grew moist

large tears rolled down her cheeks

lashes wet with tears

left hurriedly so he wouldn't see the tears running down her face

let loose a sob

let the tears come as she averted her face

lifted her *head proudly/her tear-streaked face*

lips tight with the effort to hold back tears

little tears filling the corner of her eyes

long low sob of anguish

looked on, tears moistening her eyes

lost the fight and the tears

making no secret now of the fact that she was crying

muffled a sob in his shoulder

no gentle thumb wiped her tear away

nodded, even as tears filled

nose completely stuffed from crying. She reached across to the stand beside the bed to get a tissue

not trusting herself to hold back her tears in his presence

on *a sob, she buried her face in/the verge of tears*

one hand went to *his/her* mouth as *he/she* fought back sobs

only cried and shook her head

only *then did the tears come/when he was gone did she give in to the tears*

palmed her tears away

part of him wanted to cry too

passion blazing out of his eyes

picked her up and dried the tears from her red cheeks

pressed one hand against her mouth to stifle a sob

put her hands over her face and wept like a baby

put his head in his hands and wept

quickly lowered her lashes so that he would not see the tears that sprang to her eyes

ragged *cry/sobs*

raised a tear-stained face to his

ran a curled finger under her eyes to catch the tears

ranting and screaming one minute, crying and begging the next

released a sound that was part cry, part exasperation

remembering the tears in her eyes

resting her head on his chest so he wouldn't see the tears that threatened to *fall/spill* rocking back and forth, a keening sound coming from her

roughly dashed her tears away

saw her shoulders shaking with silent sobs

scrunched her face and fought a series of sobs

set free the tears

she blinked against the hot rush of tears

she could no more contain her sobs than she could

she didn't trust her voice, not when she wanted to cry

she sighed, smiling through her tears

she sobbed his name

shook with sobs

shoulders *heaved/heaving* with sobs

shoulders shook with *emotion/unvoiced sobs*

silent tears *coursed down/dampened* her cheeks

silent tears slid from her lashes

single tear

smoothed a tear from her cheek

smoothed her hair, crooning to her until her sobs abated

sniffed back the beginning of tears

sob *lodged/rose* in her throat

sobbed and shuddered

sobbed/sobbing in his arms/incoherently/softly into her cupped hands/over the loss of

squeezed her eyes shut, fighting tears

squeezed his eyes shut *against a flood of tears/in a vain attempt to stem the tide of tears scalding his throat*

squeezed shut her eyes, commanding the tears to stay at bay

stared at him with tear filled eyes

started to cry (as he kissed her)

started to weep in earnest

steady stream of tears on her cheeks

steeled herself against another wave of tears

still sobbing as he led her away

stood looking up at him with tears in her eyes

stroked a tear from her cheek with one finger

struggled *against the hot tears burning behind her eyes/furiously against a fresh flood of tears*

struggled *against/with* the tears

struggling to hold back the hot tears that threatened to fall

suddenly on the verge of tears

swallowed a sob and squeezed *his/her* eyes shut

swallowed *and brushed away a sudden spurt of tears/back the tears*

swallowing a sob, she

swiped *at her wet cheeks/away the lingering tears*

swiping angrily at her cheeks

tear *of self-pity slid down her cheek/squeezed its way from the corner of her eye*

tears began to blur her vision

tears *blinded/blurred/blurring* her *eyes/vision* as

tears burned *at the back of his eyes/her eyes and she struggled for control*

tears *burned/of emotion welling in* her eyes

tears burst from her eyes

tears *came in earnest/fell unchecked*

tears came *to his eyes as a sense of loss enveloped him/ unbidden*

tears choked every word

tears *filled/flooded* her eyes and slid down her cheeks

tears flowing freely down her face, *whoever* turned and made her way silently back to their room

tears *formed in the corners of her eyes/mingled with laughter*

tears gathered and overflowed in her eyes, but these were tears of happiness

tears *glistened in/instantly filled* her eyes as

tears of *joy sprang to her eyes/pain and rage/relief nearly blinded her*

tears *pooled in his/rushed to her* eyes

tears rivered down her cheeks

tears *rolled/slipped* silently down her cheeks

tears rushed from the depths of her tortured soul

tears *slipping over her cheeks/spilling in happiness/spiked her lashes*

tears *spilled/spilling* over *and ran down his face/her spiked lower lashes/their cheeks*

tears *sprang anew/spread* to her eyes

tears *sting/stung* her eyes

tears streamed in a silent path down her face

tears stung her eyes but she valiantly fought them

tears swimming in her eyes

tears *that stained her/trickled down her* cheeks

tears threatened at the thought of leaving *wherever/whoever*

tears threatened to *fall/flow*, but she held them in

tears threatening to swell over

tears welled up behind her lids, but her anger kept the tears at bay

tears were now openly flowing down her cheeks

tears weren't far away however

the anguish in *whoever's* cry tore through *whoever's* soul

the hot press of tears threatened

the sad lament of the music drifted to her ears and brought tears to her eyes

the *silent tears of defeat/tears came again, in a flood this time*

the sobs she fought to suppress shook her delicate frame

the tears came *hard/now, hot and fast and bitter*

the tears *poured down her cheeks faster than she could swipe them away/spilling down her face left her without words*

the urge to burst into tears overwhelmed her, but she

the word caught on a sob

the words *dissolved into incoherent sobs/tears*

then and only then did she let fall the tears that had threatened

threw herself into his arms, crying softly against his *tunic/shirt*

throat squeezing tight with *grief/recollection/unshed tears*

through *her ragged sobs/tear-soaked lashes/the blur of tears*

thumbed *away her tear/the tears from her cheeks*

too exhausted to cry anymore

tried to choke back the tears

trying to stifle a cry

turned away to hide her own tears

unable to restrain herself, she let the tears fall silently

unbridled tears flowed freely

unexpected/unshed tears *glistened in/sprang to* her eyes

voice *choked with emotion/cracked with tears*

voice *dissolved into hysterical tears/trailed away with a choked sob*

was helpless to stop the tears

was *on the verge of/suddenly close to* tears

was trying not to cry, but her vision was already blurred

wept bitter, hopeless tears

when her storm of tears abated

when she got control of herself she wiped her tears from

when she looked up at him her eyes glittered with tears

whispered the plea through a mist of tears

wiped *a curled forefinger beneath her eye/away a lingering tear*

wiped her tears away gently

wiping away *a tear and steeling her courage/tears that threatened to fall, she*

wiping her tears

with a quick swipe she wiped away her tears
with a ragged cry she turned and ran
with one tender finger, he stroked a stray tear from her face
with sobs and sweeping gestures
words dissolved into a sob

Create Your Own Tags!

~

5

LIMBS – ARMS, LEGS, HANDS, FEET, SHOULDERS

A. Hands

~

clenched her fists angrily at her sides

closed his eyes and tried to still his trembling hands

closed the space between them, catching her hands within his

could hardly keep his hands off her

crooked his finger

dragged *a hand over his face/an unsteady hand through his hair*

drummed his fingers on the table

eased his fingers between hers

elbows and hands flying in all directions

enormous hands with long, graceful fingers

felt *his/her* hand shake as

finger gently trailed down her face with the faintest touch

fingers *brushed her/flexed against her thighs/kept flexing/ intertwined with her own/like iron bands/moved/stiff with cold/threaded into her hair/tightened around his hand/trembled*

fingers sliding up into the soft waves of his hair

fingers surrounded her forearm in an iron *grasp/grip*

fingers tightened around the handle of his knife

fingers traveled down her back in a bold manner

fist couldn't have landed with greater impact

fisted her hands *against her hips/in her skirts, willing herself to breathe evenly*

fisted/fisting his hands until the nails cut into his palms

fists *clenched at his sides/flying to her hips*

fit his hand around the jeweled hilt

folded her *cold, trembling hands between his warm fingers/hands and tried hard not to lose her temper*

forced her trembling hands to stillness

fought to control the tremor that overtook her hands

gathered her slender hands within his

gave a *dismissive wave of her hand/squeeze to her hand*

had strong hands, and his fingers felt warm and comforting

hadn't laid a hand on her, yet the sting of his words was tantamount to a slap

hand *at her throat/captured her/*

hand *curled into a helpless fist/disappeared within his larger one*

hand *fell reflexively to her belly/frail and lifeless to the touch*

hand *grazed her breast/held captive in his/moved weakly*

hand *still trembled/trembled as*

hand came up, fingers gently lifting her chin

hand shot out and *caught her wrist/slapped her*

hand skimmed her jaw, slid down her throat, came to rest on her breast

hands clenched *in/into tight* fists

hands like bands of steel clamped around her arms

hands *rose to grip her bare shoulders/roved restlessly over her back*

hands *slid slowly down her hips/so small tucked in his*

hands *steepled together/tightly clasped in his lap*

hands *shook and she knotted them into fists/whitened around*

hands *skimmed her body/tightened over her shoulders*

hands trembled as she opened *the missive/whatever*

hands *tucked and folded on her lap/were shaking as*

hands were sweating and her heart pounded beneath her *chest/(rose/whatever-colored) bodice*

he seized her wrist

he stood, leaning forward, hands braced on the desk

held her hands together so tightly they began to shake

held her head in her hands and cried

held it loosely in her gnarled fingers

held out *her hands, palms up/his hands in welcome*

held two fingers against her mouth in contemplation

her eyes kept returning to the clasped hands she held rigidly on her lap

her hands *balled into fists/shook uncontrollably*

her hands *held serenely at her waist/on her ample hips*

her hands, only skin over bones, trembled

her nervous hands betrayed her agitation

her palms were damp as

hiding a smile behind *his/her* hand

his hand *clamped hard upon her arm/closed firmly around her wrist*

his hand lifted and fell

his hand lingered at the small of her back, the gesture both steadying and possessive

his hand on the back of her head anchoring it in place

his hand shot out, captured her wrist and yanked her close

his hands *clenched into throbbing fists/stilled*

his hands closed around her upper arms to steady her

his hands shot out to clamp around her upper arms, his grip just short of painful

his large hands spanned her waist

hit her with his open hand

holding her hand *longer than the required handshake/up she used her fingers to mimic a yapping mouth*

hooked a thumb at the door

jabbed/jabbing a/his finger *at her/in his direction*

joined his hands behind him as he strolled *beside/along* the

keep your hands off my *woman/things/whatever*, he said in a deadly whisper

knotted her hands into fists, fighting for self-control

laid *a comforting hand on her arm/his hand upon hers*

lifted her hand to strike him, but he caught it easily

looked at her hands, then looked up at him

looked at her over steepled fingers

loved the gentleness of his hands

made an impatient gesture with his hand

pain in her hands made her realize she had gripped the *whatever* with a death grip

placed her hands in her lap so no one would know how they trembled

planted her *fists/hands* on her hips and glared at him

pointed *a gnarled finger at/over his shoulder tow*ard

pointed at her, emphasizing each word with a stab of his finger

put a shaky hand on his shoulder

put her hand *on her chest to still her breathing/over her plump bosom*

put her hands on the table to steady herself

putting *his/her* chin on her hands

rammed his hands into his pockets

ran gnarled, toil-worn hands over the

reached *down for her hands to help her stand/out a hand to stop her, but she evaded him*

reaching for her hand and cutting her off

released her hand with an effusive apology

rested *her chin on her knees/her hands on his chest/his chin against steepled fingers*

rested her *hands/palms against/upon* his chest and could feel his heart beating

rough hands seized *him/her*

rubbed the tension from *his/her* jaw with *his/her* hand

rubbing *his/her* hands together to ensure they were warm
scrubbed *a hand/his hands roughly* over his face
seized her hand and pulled her to
set her hands on his lapel
settled his *hand on her arm to comfort her/hands on his hips*
shaking *his/her* finger in admonishment
shook off *his/her* restraining hand
slapped his hand hard on her rump
slid his hand over her fingers, anchoring her hand to his arm
slipped her hand into his
smacked his hand away
spanned her waist with his strong hands
spread her hands in surrender
squeezed *her hand in support/his hand, his grip weak*
stayed her with a hand
steadying her hands she
stood and dusted off *his/her* hands
stretched *her neck to gain a view of/out his hand in welcome*
stretched out with his hands locked behind his head
striking him with her fists
strong, capable fingers cupped her face and turned it up to his
struggled to pull free, but his hands held her fast
swept his hand wide
swept *whatever* from her hands
templed his fingers in thought
the feeling of his warm, calloused hand holding hers left her
the fingers of his *right/left* hand rubbed against the thumb
the *frantic clutch of her hands/light touch of his fingers*
the strength *in his hands and arms/of his unyielding grip*
there was ownership in his touch
threw both hands in the air *in mock surrender/as if he gave up on*

threw her hands up in the air, displaying her total disgust

threw him a *bewildered look/look of distaste*

threw his hand, palm forward, in the air

threw off his hands, shuddering at his touch

took both her hands in his

took her hand and *held/squeezed* it and she didn't pull it away

traced his *fingers along his clean-shaven jaw/hand down her face*

traced his *fingers over her smooth shoulders/jawline with her forefinger*

wagged his index finger at her

wanted to slam his fist through the table or into this unknown man's chin

waved a hand before she could finish

waved his *hand dismissively/wife into silence*

with *shaking hands/shaky fingers* she

worried her ring around her finger

you have your mother's hands

B. Shoulders

*~

a creaking sound made him look over his shoulder

a shiver danced across her shoulders

arm circled her shoulders and he eased her against his chest

arms *and shoulders ached/twined about his broad shoulders*

arms that felt as strong as steel shifted her weight so her head lay against his broad shoulder

back and shoulders ached

bellowed over his shoulder

braced his hand above her shoulders, effectively pinning her against the door

came to him, touched his shoulder lightly

cast a narrow-eyed glance over his shoulder

casting her over his shoulder with ease

caught her by the shoulders and dragged her against him

caution made her look over her shoulder again

clapped *him/her* warmly on the *shoulder/back*

coming close to put a hand on her *shoulder/back*

could feel the tension between his shoulder blades

curling a hand over her shoulder

defeat *held no honor/weighed heavy on her shoulders*

draping his arm possessively around her shoulders

drew in a deep breath and squared her shoulders

dropped *her shoulders in defeat/his hands and moved away*

explored the contours of his muscled shoulders and back

felt a burden lifted from her shoulders found herself hefted over his shoulder

gave him a shoulder hug

gently *seized her elbow/touched her shoulder*

grabbed her shoulders *in a grip so tight she flinched/and turning her around*

grasped her shoulders with fingers of steel

guilt weighing on his shoulders

hair had fallen around her shoulders

hands *clutched his shoulders/linked behind his head*

hands *returned to her lap/gripped her shoulder to steady her*

hard hands grabbed her shoulders

he caught her shoulders, shook her roughly

he lifted a shoulder

head nestled against his shoulder

held her shoulders, looking into her eyes

her frail shoulders *falling/slumping* in surrender

her gaze settled on his shoulders, which shifted under his shirt as he moved

her misery weighed heavily on his shoulders

her *palms/hands* moved over his hard shoulders

her shoulders *drooped/stiffened*

her shoulders *slumping in defeat/uncharacteristically slumped*

his *breadth of shoulder/broad shoulders strained the seams of his*

his hand gripped her shoulder, imparting wordless comfort

his hand on her shoulder kept her silent

his hand on her shoulder, he

his hands *caressed her shoulders/placed proprietarily on her shoulders*

his massive shoulders

his shoulders were rigid, his hands clenched at his sides

his somber gaze on some point just beyond *whoever's* shoulders

kept her shoulders back and her chin raised as if readying herself for battle

laid *her cheek against his shoulder/*his hand upon her shoulder and squeezed

leaned *a/his* shoulder against the *jamb/wall*

leaned his shoulder into the nearest wall, his eyes never leaving hers

lifted a frail shoulder

lifted her chin and *squared her shoulders/straightened her back*

lifted her *into his strong arms/trembling fingers and*

lifted one shoulder *in a half shrug/wearily*

lifted his shoulders in a *casual/wry* shrug

lifting her so her head rested against his shoulder

merely shrugged his broad shoulders

neck and shoulders bristled with tension

nodded knowingly and clamped a hand on his shoulder

offered a helpless lift of one shoulder

picked her up and tossed her unceremoniously over his shoulder

playfully slapped his shoulder

pleased by the revelation, his shoulders relaxed

poked his shoulder hard

put his hand on her shoulder. Marking his territory?

reached over his shoulder and plucked an arrow from the quiver

regret drooping *his/her* shoulders

rested her forehead on his shoulder as her tears soaked through his shirt

rising, he touched her shoulders

rolled his shoulders

settled *a hand anxiously upon his shoulder/his arm around the too-thin shoulders*

shawl clung to her shoulders like a lover's fingers

shifting his burden to his other shoulder

shoved the heels of her hands against his shoulders

shrugged *and looked away/as she sipped her Sherry*

shrugged *indifferently/without answering*

shrugged clear of his hand and opened the door

shrugged *his broad/off the hand on his* shoulders

slapping him on the back, cuffing him on the shoulder

slipping an arm around her shoulders

some of the tension eased in her shoulders

squared her shoulders and *lifted/jutted* her chin

squared/squaring her shoulders *defiantly/she lifted her chin*

squeezed her hands together, then collected herself and squared her shoulders

standing her ground, she squared her shoulders

startled and glanced over her shoulder

stole a *glance over her shoulder/sideways glance at him*

straightened her shoulders and raised her chin

strode over to her and gripped her shoulders, willing her to understand, yet unable to explain

strong, steady shoulder whenever she needed him to be

tall, broad-shouldered man

the blow jarred his arm to his shoulder

the breadth of his *chest/shoulders*

the coat stretched across his broad shoulders

the gentleness in the hand that dropped onto her shoulder

the hands gripping her shoulders pulled her close

the set of his shoulders

the tension *filled/left* his neck and shoulders

the weight *of the world on his shoulders/on her chest increased*

took her by the shoulders as if to shake her and then lowered his hands

tossed a grin over his broad shoulder

unexpected feelings of comfort and tranquility draped themselves around her shoulders like a favorite well-worn robe

warm arms wrapped around her shoulders

weariness *showed in her slumped/weighted her* shoulders

wide shoulders, arms thick with muscle

with her shoulders set stiffly back

worry had weighed upon his shoulders

wrapped an affectionate arm across her shoulder

wrapped his arms around her *heaving shoulders/waist*

C. Arms

~

argued, attempting to wrest her arm free

arm curled around the small of her back, pulling her to him

arm slipped around her waist, crushing her tighter to him

arm/leg was still useless

arms *corded with thick muscles/fell limply at her sides*

arms crossed over his bare, muscular chest, foot tapping impatiently

arms *held tight around his knees/laden with/tightened*

circled in the strength of his arms

cried and fell into his open arms

crossed arms smugly over his chest

crossed his muscled arms in front of him and leaned against the

crossing her arms for warmth

drew her *back to/slowly into his arms*

enfolding her in his arms

flung herself at him (into his arms)

folded his arms over his massive chest

gave her *arm a quick supportive squeeze/fingers a gentle squeeze*

gave her *hand another/shoulder a familiar* squeeze

grabbed her elbow, pulling her alongside him

gripped her more tightly in his arms

gripped his neck with his forearm, holding him in choke hold

growing boldness in his arms pleased him

he opened his arms. She flew into them

he paced back and forth, his arms locked behind his back

he seized her firmly but gently by her upper arms

held her tight, his arms almost crushing her

held her upper arm in a punishing grip

held out his arms *in silent invitation/and she came to him*

her arms longing to cradle

his arms refusing to loose his precious captive

his arms tightened around her until she could scarcely breathe

his fingers bit into her arms so hard they would certainly leave marks

his *massive/powerful* arms tightening around her like a vise

his strong arms holding her protectively

huge arms straining as he pulled, jerking his arm free

jabbed hard with her good arm

kept his arm around her in a protective manner

lifted her in his strong arms and held her against his chest linked her arm companionably with

longed to fling her arms around his neck, hug him, reassure him that everything would be all right

longed to hold her in his arms

made *an effort to slip from his arms/no move to take her in his arms*

moved *among the guests/aside to let her through it*

moved *drunkenly about the room/gingerly/her into his arms*

moved to fling her arms around him, but stopped herself just in time

muscled arms covered with a sheen of sweat

nearly collapsing into his arms

once he held her in his arms, rational thought had fled

opened her arms in welcome

put *a comforting arm around her/her arms around his waist for balance*

put his arms around her *shoulders/wanting to give her comfort*

putting *a firm arm around/his arm behind her back for support*

reached *for her/out and touched him*

reached out and grabbed her *arm/hand*, pulling her close

reached out impulsively and touched *his/her* arm

reached out to *gently squeeze her upper arms/steady herself against*

rested contentedly in the circle of his arms, her head against his shoulder, blinking hard

rivulets of water dripped down his corded arms and chest

rubbed *her arms briskly/his sweaty hands together/the thin skin of her hand*

rushed to wrap her in his arms

she should resist him, but her arms crept up and around his neck

she *stiffened in the circle of/stood woodenly in* his arms

slid her arm about her friend's trembling shoulders

stepped around him but was yanked back when he gripped her arm

strolled with their arms around each other

strong arms pulled him back seconds before the roof collapsed

strong arms snaking around her waist

swept her behind him with his other arm

the muscles in his *arms were tense and corded/jaw working*

the muscles in his biceps swelled as he crossed his arms over his naked chest

the muscles in his upper arms strained

the muscular arms cradling her

threw herself into his open arms

tightened his arm around her waist

tried to pull away from him, but his grip tightened

tried to slip from his arms, but he held her in place

unable to bear her sorrow, he pulled her into his arms and held her

walking *arm in arm/hand in hand/side by side they/with linked arms*

was determined to have her willing in his arms

waved her *back into her seat/concerns aside*

waved his words away as if they had no meaning

waved *in farewell/off the compliment*

waved the men into an abrupt silence

went into his welcoming arms

when she was in his arms it felt like the safest place she could be

when the horror had been too much, he had lifted her into his arms

without giving her any warning he scooped her up into his arms

wrapped a steely arm around her

wrapped her arms around *her knees/herself*

wrapped her arms around him, needing something solid to hang on to wrapped her in the warm safety of his *embrace/both of his arms*

wrenched her arm free

D. Legs

~

a sudden surge of weariness flooded him and he had to fight to stay on his feet

a sure stride straight toward

as she padded in on bare feet, he turned around and smiled at

barely made it upstairs on her shaking legs

booted feet stomping *away from/toward her*

bounded/sprang to *his/her* feet

could barely make her legs move

crossed the room with purposeful strides

crossing one booted leg over the other

disembarked on wobbly legs

effortlessly matching her steps

fearing her legs would collapse at any moment

feet *felt rooted to the floor/were dragging/were getting numb*

felt her *knees tremble/stop struggling in his arms*

folded his arms and crossed his legs at the ankle

forced herself to walk as normally as possible

gained *his/her* feet

gait slow and determined

gritting her teeth when her feet touched the ground

he came at once to his feet

he lost patience, cursed under his breath and rose to his feet

he *lumbered over/merely shrugged/nodded once*

he quickly gained his feet

he should turn away. Should leave. But something held his feet in place

her feet nearly buckled beneath her when her feet hit the ground

her hip brushed his

her knees *buckled and he caught her/quaking as she tried to walk*

her legs *and feet entwined with his/burning with exhaustion*

her legs *nearly buckled/propelled her forward*

her legs *so rubbery with terror/turned to water*

his knees nearly buckled

his leg had stiffened while he'd been seated

hobbled *along to keep up/past him/to*

hobbled off and quickly disappeared into the crowd

hoisted her to her feet

hooked her arms under her legs and swung them over the side of the bed

hooking one arm around her back and the other beneath her knees

hurried on silent feet

I'm not walking to *him/the next town, etc.* I'm just walking away from you

knee brushed hers

kneecaps turned to jelly

kneeling before her, he gathered her icy hands in his warm ones

kneeling on one knee, he slipped an arm around her waist to support her weight

knees began to buckle. He caught her before she could fall

knees *felt weak/nearly buckled with relief*

knees were so wobbly it's a wonder she could stand up at all

leapt to her feet, a cry upon her lips

leapt wearily to her feet

leg *cocked on a bench/was badly fractured*

leg tucked up under her ~ sitting

legs astride, sword drawn

legs buckled and she went down hard

legs *weakened as/went weak*

legs wobbled *as she stood/like jelly*

lengthened his strides

levered himself to his feet and

long strides rapidly closing the space

long, muscular legs displayed to advantage

long, *purposeful strides/shapely legs*

made her way *quietly downstairs/up the stairs*

made her way toward *wherever/whoever* on steady feet

moving slowly on leaden feet, he

moving upon legs that threatened to give way beneath him, he staggered

moving with an easy gait

not giving heed to the time, she jumped to her feet and

not going to run very far on that foot

on unsteady legs

paced a few steps in one direction and then the other

paced *about in her frustration/away her frustrations*

paced *back and forth before/impatiently*

paced the room *restlessly/with long strides, his breath measured*

pacing *angrily he/the room, a troubled look on his face*

padded *barefoot back to the bed/down the stairs in her bare feet*

pushed himself to his feet with noticeable effort

rested his forearms across his thighs

rose and *drew her to her feet/took both her hands*

rose in a single, lithe motion

rose stiffly from *his/her* chair

rose to *go to her/her feet in delight/his feet in one smooth motion*

rose to greet his guest, a friendly grin curving his lips as he clutched the other man's hand in greeting

sat back and pulled one knee up to his chest

sat in the chair since her legs no longer seemed capable of support scrambled awkwardly to her feet

she ordered her feet to move, but they wouldn't listen

she'd curled a leg under herself to sit on the

shifted his weight from one foot to the other, looking uncomfortable

shuffled his feet, looking uncomfortable

slammed to his feet

staggered *backward/to his feet*

standing *about in small clutches/and yanking her to her feet*

standing in *his imposing shadow/the opening (door)*

standing *perilously close/stock still/up and offering her his hand*

stilled her feet

stood up *and walked around the room/slowly, her legs unsteady*

stood, her legs shaky

stretched his legs, one ankle over the other

strides *relentless/were long and formidable*

striding through the

strode away with grim determination and purpose

strode toward the building, heedless of the danger

strode up the drive and rapped firmly on the door

strong *legs carried him to the stable/pair of arms/powerful legs*

struggled on weak legs

stumbled *and nearly fell/from the room/to her feet*

swayed on her feet

swinging her legs to the floor

that reached to his feet

there was dead silence for a minute, followed by rushing feet

threw back the covers and swung her legs out of the bed

throwing his legs over the side of the bed and rushing to the door

thrust to his feet

turned a slow circle, taking in her surroundings

unsteady on her feet

walked a *few steps before answering/little farther in silence*

walked *along the water's edge/blindly through/calmly and with purpose*

walked *companionably to/gingerly toward*

walked alongside her husband, feeling small and insignificant

walked *back to the house in silence/briskly down the long corridor*

walked in *silence for a few moments/together*

walked *in terrified silence as/on in companionable silence*

walked out on legs that were trembling

walked over, a serious expression on his face

walked *slowly across the room and slowed at/stiffly past*

walked to the door and pulled on her gloves

walked toward her slowly, *his features masked/purposefully*

walked toward *him/her* with confidence

walked with *a determined purpose/determined steps to*

walking *off the aftereffects/toward her with a slow predatory grace*

walks out into the bright sunlight

warily she rose to her feet

warmth slowly being restored to her hands and feet as he settled

was no match for his long-legged stride/on his feet by then

when she thought her legs wouldn't hold her again

Whoever had cut her feet in several places while being dragged along

wrenching her to her feet

6

ROOM DÉCOR/FURNITURE/BUILDINGS

*~

a bare table (green baize)

a breeze fluttered the curtains

a huge bed that dominated the room

a large, black lacquered wardrobe stood against one wall

and the finest and handsomest table

as he hunkered down next to her chair

banged one clenched fist on the table, setting cups and saucers to rattling

blazed with candles

book lined shelves filled the far wall

book-lined walls

candlelight flickering

candles glow warmly

carpets added warmth to a room

chandelier casting a prism of light

chintz covered sofa

closed off cooking area

crossed the room and sat down in the chair adjacent

crossed to his favorite leather chair

crystal crashed and splintered

curled up in a chair

deep *green/whatever color* damask curtains framed the wide windows

downed a gulp and returned the cup to the table

dropped down onto the padded chair with a whoosh of breath

dropped into the chair with a thud

eased her tired bones back into the old rocker

flagstone floor

floor-to-ceiling bookshelves

flung open the heavy, solid oak door

got up and paced to the glass doors

grabbed hold of the nearest chair to steady himself

gripped the edge of the table

ground his cigar butt in a crystal ashtray

handsome mahogany desk

he pulled a straight chair around, propped his foot on the seat, and leaning forward, rested his forearms on his thigh

he quit the *chamber/room/house*

her fingers dug into the arms of her invalid chair

high, barrel-vaulted ceiling

his fingers drummed against the table

his fist crashed down on the table

his footsteps muffled by the thick carpet

his girth spilled over the edges of the *chair/whatever he was sitting on*

his large frame dwarfed the *chair/room*

its steeple gleaming like a beacon (*church/kirk*)

knife clattered on the table

lace curtains billowing

leaned back in his chair, tapped long fingers on the side of his tea glass

leaned back in the chair and pressed his fingertips together

leather chair behind the desk

leather-bound books lined the whole of one wall

long table set up with refreshments

maneuvered his chair to a spot a discreet distance from where the two embraced

mantle clock chimed the hour

mullioned panes of glass

papers strewn across his desk

Persian carpets covered the floor

pillows plump with goose down

placed his palms on the desk and pushed himself up from the chair

placed the lamp on a side table near the bed

pounding a fist upon the table

pulling out a chair and spinning it around to straddle the seat

punched the pillow in fury

punched up the bed pillows to his satisfaction and

pushed aside the dark *blue/green/whatever color* damask curtain

pushed away from the table

Queen Anne wing chairs arranged in front of the fire

rested *a hand on the newel post/his arms on the table*

rested his elbow on the table and cupped his chin

rich farmstead

rich oak paneling

rocked in the chair

rocker ~ slow, easy back and forth rhythm

rose from his chair and came around the desk to sit on its edge

rounding the table in slow motion

sank *back in a/onto the* chair

sank slowly on to the bed

sat back *broodingly in his chair/in her chair, dumbfounded*

sat on the *whatever furniture* and made a pretense of arranging her skirt

sat on their bed feeling empty

sat up straighter in his *oxblood leather/whatever kind of chair* and pinned *whoever* with a glare

setting the deserted buildings on fire

settled *back against/in his chair and tented his fingers*

settled himself on the chair

settled into the tub, his bones creaking in tired protest

shadows danced upon the wall

shoes clattering on the bare *oak/whatever* steps

shouted and slammed his hand down on the table

shoved *at the door/back his chair and rose*

shoved away his plate, his appetite already gone

shoved the door wide and swept in on a gust of wind and rain

shrugged and dropped into a chair behind the desk

slouched in his chair, stretching out his long legs

slumped back into his chair, his eyes drifting wearily shut

sparse furnishings

sprang out of bed with an agile leap

started up from the chair

straddling the seat, he sat and rested his arms on the back of the chair

struck his fist against the table in a bitter rage

swatted his napkin against the table

tapestry covered chair

the *buttery soft leather/food-laden table*

the far end of the hall enveloped by shadows

the firelight cast his profile into stern planes and hid his eyes in shadow

the pattern on the old wedding ring quilt

the room *bathed in warmth and soft firelight/full of shadows*

the room *seemed to shrink in on her/snug and welcoming*

the room softly lit by the glow of a dying fire

the room they were in was furnished in dark woods and soft blue and green fabrics

the room's opulence

the *table was scored and darkened with use/tables groaned with*

the ticking of the clock on the mantel

the wide bed was covered with

to the formal dining room where myriads of flickering candles graced the table and wall sconces

took off his glasses and leaned back in his chair

tossed his hat to a side table

we sit down together, we get up together

went down on one knee beside the chair

worn wood floors

worn, weary buildings lined the streets

7

MISCELLANEOUS

~

crawled into the bed and sat with her back against the headboard

held her, half supporting her as she collapsed against him, rocking her gently, stroking her hair, her back in soothing, healing motions

her chest tightened

jutted a hip

laid his hand on the small of her back and steered her into

long lean frame

numbness deadened her limbs

paused to shake her head

prodded at her back

she squeezed her eyes tighter, fought to control the sudden trembling of her limbs

stretched a moment and worked the kinks from his back

the feel of his hard torso as he held her in his arms

turned her back on him

turned his head, bringing his face so close

warm water soothed her limbs

willing what strength he could into his limbs

8

ANGER

~

a *blind fury swept through his/cry of fury went up among*

a dark *rage contorting his handsome features/scowl* on

a dark storm gathering in his eyes

a fist of potent fury

a flicker of contempt crossed his features

a low angry voice startled her

a muscle ticked in his jaw, the only outward manifestation of his *anger/fury*

a quiet rage began to simmer within him

a red haze of anger filled his mind

a red-hot rage shot through him

a roar bursting from his throat

a sick sense of fury

a spark of anger lit his eyes

accepting his anger as his due

air heavy with her anger

allowing the anger and hatred to seep through her

an angry *outburst followed/scowl across his face*

anger and *disappointment/rage*

anger *bubbled up and welled over/causing his face to flush*

anger charged through her. She marched over to him and jabbed a finger into his chest

anger *coiled through her body/flared in his eyes*

anger flashed across his *face/features*

anger *hung in the air/in his eyes*

anger laced her words
anger *mounting/surged anew*
anger rose for a moment, but he tamped it down
anger, hot and molten
anger/hatred/fear lending her strength
anger/rage festered within his mind
angered beyond reason and filled with rage
angrily attacked him with a blow to the head
angry and no longer trying to hide it
angry color rose in *his/her* face
angry exchange
angry rebuff served only to incense him further
angry *tears well in her eyes/with herself for*
angry, his eyes darkened to flint
anguish in her *soul/heart*
animosity grew to hatred
apparently you're still angry. I'm past angry. I'm done
barely suppressed fury in his voice
baring his teeth with savage fury
beamed his pleasure
beat back the anger that flared within him
been angry and jealous—and afraid
between anger and anxiety
bit *back her anger/her lip with frustrated rage*
blue/whatever color eyes filled with fury
body shaking *in anger/with rage*
body tense with anger
bristling with fury
brushed them away with angry, impatient fingers
choked *back his anger/out with a mixture of shock and anger*

clenched his jaw and fought to control the anger welling within him

closed the distance between them, feeling the anger *rising/rise up* within him

closed the space between them in a few angry strides

cold *fury glittered in their depths/rage settled on him*

cold, angry eyes

controlled anger

couldn't keep the anger out of his voice

crazy jealousy and raged

cried *brokenly/fiercely*

crossed to her with angry strides

dark *angry flashes/fury etching the lines of his face*

didn't *bother masking his anger/flinch from the fury in them*

drawing in a huge gasp of outrage

dread *builds/chilled his blood*

dread *flashed through/seized/washed over* her

dread was swiftly replaced with anger

dreaded the thought that

enraged, he bolted upright

every muscle in his/her body quivering with rage

exploded with fury

express their rage and frustration

eyes *black with fury/blazed/blazing*

eyes bright with *hate/indignity and anger*

eyes burned with a hatred so strong *she feared for her life/her blood ran cold*

eyes darkening with rage

eyes *flared/glinted/snapped* with fury

eyes flashed with *anger/temper*

eyes glinted with *contempt/malice*

eyes glittered with silent fury

face contorted with anger

face dark with hatred

face darkened with rage

face *filled with anger/grew harder*

face flushed *red with fury/with heat and anger*

face held *such/turned white with* fury

face twisted into an ugly mask of hatred

face was black with outrage

faces filled with anger and distrust

features tight with rage

feeling a growing sense of outrage

feelings of rage and frustration

felt *a sudden fury/an icy rage*

felt betrayed and *angry/compelled to*

felt the *anger shimmering off him/fury of their bloodlust*

fighting to put aside his anger

fills with rage as he listens to *whomever* recount her ordeal with her father

fingers curled into his palm as his anger grew (into a fist)

forced down his anger

fought *against a rush of anger/desperately to control the fury*

fought down a *tide/rise* of anger

fought to keep the anger from his voice

frustration *etched itself across/welled within*

frustration *fueled his anger/made her furrow her brow*

fury *against/boiled inside him*

fury bristled from every inch of her

fury *burned through her/burning in his eyes*

fury *clouded/darkened/mottled* his face

fury *contorted/danced across* his features

fury coursed through his veins

fury *engulfed/radiated from* him

fury escalated with each fruitless encounter

fury *pulsed/roiled* through *him/her*

fury rose in her eyes

fury *seizing him/surged through his veins*

fury simmered to a boil

fury *turned his eyes nearly black/twisted his features*

fury, anguish and *the/an* ever-present tug of war inside him threatened to

gasped in outrage

girding herself with anger she

grappling with his anger

grief and rage clutched at his gut

ground out a sound of anger and impatience

halted his angry invective

hasn't he enough fuel to his anger already?

he *brooded/swung around in fury*

he was angry. Very angry

he was *enraged/truly angry*

he/she stared at *him/her*, feeling a sudden rise of fury

he'd nursed his anger and hate for so long

he'd piqued an anger in her she thought she'd buried beyond reach

held back his anger

her anguish

her eyes were hard with bitterness

her lovely *blue/green/whatever color* eyes snapping with anger

her thoughts raged

his anger leaves her feeling unsettled

his anger lent steadiness to his steps

his anger *remained, unabated/spilled over*

his angry face glaring down on her

his bellow of outrage reverberated off the

his blood simmered with wrath

his *chin clamped in anger/eyes flashed cold-blue fury*

his eyes flicked over him in ill-concealed contempt

his face darkened with *anger/fury*, and she hurried on with her story

his face *flushed dark with anger/grew thunderous*

his face mottled with fury

his face *suddenly darkened in/the embodiment of* rage

his fury like an electric charge in the room

his fury nearly blinded him

his jaw *clenched/clenching* in anger

his jaw *clenched involuntarily/firmed/set tightly*

his jaw *hard/hardened*

his lips thinned *in anger/with frustration*

his mouth a thin line of anger

his nostrils flared in outrage

his piercing *blue/green/gray* eyes hardened with anger

his posture rigid, his fury barely contained

his tone, his demeanor were cold and angry

his voice *dropped low and menacing/*edged with fury he couldn't hide

his voice laced with fury and self-control

his voice lethally *restrained/soft*

his voice was quiet, but she caught the note of fury underneath

holding her fury in check

holding up her hands to ward off his rage

huffed out an angry breath

hurt and outrage swelled

I'm here to help. Why are you so angry?

ice/fury edged her words

if you need to be angry with someone, be angry with me

impotent rage roared through him

in an attempt to control his rising fury

in blind fury

in the face of his fury, she

in the *grip of an icy rage/heat of her anger*

intervened before his ire could come to a full boil

irrational fury flooded through him

irritation *bubbled to the surface/ripe in his voice/surged through her*

it amused him to see

it still angered him that

jaw *clenched to hold back angry words/tight with anger*

like a fire burning through dry wood, the anger threatened to consume him

listened to him with rising fury

looked at him *unhappily/with unbridled fury*

made a low, angry sound

moved to anger, he

murderous rage roiling inside him

no attempt to hide his anger

obviously still furious with her

outraged all over again

own anger rose again

pain and anger in her voice

pinned him with an angry look

provoked to fury

pushed down *his/her* anger at the idea of

rage *boiled in her/nearly blinded him*

rage *burned dark and hot in his eyes/flared her senses*

rage choked him, and he began once more to pace restlessly about the room

rage *heated his face/returned in a bitter surge*
rage *roared/surged* through her
rage rushed through him, energizing him
rage seething closer to the surface
raged *at/silently/with impatience*
raw fury *filled/welled up inside him*
reeling from their angry comments
released him with a grunt of muted fury
said with utter fury
said, barely able to control his anger
savage roar of fury
saw the fury that gripped
schooled his angry features
scowled *at her/in anger*
seemed irritated
seethed with impotent rage
seething with rage and betrayal
seething, she
sensed his fury
set his blood boiling with rage
settled back happily
shaking with *anger/fury* as
shame and fury
she raged
should have been cowering before his anger, yet
shouted with sudden fury
shrieked in outrage
sick and outraged
silent and angry, he
skewered him with an *angry/fiery* glare
skin flushed with anger

spare me the outrage. It rings false coming from you

sparks of anger

spat the words as he jerked his head toward

speared her with an angry gaze

sputtered in *anger/outrage*

squeezed her hand and fought down his anger

stiffened with fury

stood still, fighting his rage

struggled to *contain his fury/tamp down his rage*

sudden surge of anger battled within

suppressed a surge of rage

surprise and bafflement giving way to anger

swallowed hard against his barely suppressed anger

swung around on a surge of anger

swung around, pinning her with an angry glare

talked him down out of his rage

tense with anger

that angers me

the anger had left him, and the dull feeling of emptiness he lived with each day had come in

the anger in his eyes wasn't to be dismissed lightly

the anguish and fury she was experiencing

the early signs of rage

the flash of rage that flared through him

the fury *he barely held in check/in her eyes defying him to touch her again*

the *haze of anger lifted/leashed fury in him*

the look of *fury on his face/hatred between them* as he stalked toward her

the scowl on his face matched his angry words

the sight served to soften his fury

the worry he'd felt only moments before dissolved into anger then came the confusion and anger

tight lips and snapping eyes betrayed his fury

tightened his jaw in fury

too angry at this point to speak

trembling with suppressed rage

tried to shut out the sound of his rage

trying *her best to soothe his anger/to keep her anger in check*

trying to avoid the throngs of angry men in the street

trying to tamp the anger *he'd/she'd* held simmering all day

turned and smiled at him as he entered the room

twisted and writhed in fury

understand that you're angry

unleashed her wrath

visibly *outraged/upset*

voice dropped low and dangerous, his *whatever color* eyes snapping with rage

voice held traces of fury

voice was deadly quiet above the roar of fury in his head

voice was *taut/tight* with *anger/fury*

volcanic rage

waged an angry war inside

was *angry and tired/rigid and trembling with outrage*

was so angry she couldn't speak

was working himself into a terrible anger

watched his tall, angry shape recede

why is he angry with me? He isn't. He's angry with himself. He couldn't protect her

willed his anger to burn off before returning to the work at hand

with a *growl/snarl* of rage

with a snarl, he shoved her atway from him

with an angry shake of his head

you're angry, and I understand. I won't try to argue with you

9

FROWNING

*~

a frown *crossed her face/marred her normally cheerful countenance*

a *perplexed frown creasing her forehead/worried frown on his face*

a slight frown *furrowed his brows for a moment/marred her face, then disappeared*

asked frowning, obviously annoyed

brows furrowed, he directed his frown at her

deepened her frown

faint frown on his face

from the frown lines on his face it was evident that

frown *deepened/drawing* her lips down

frowned and looked down at her gloved hands

frowned as she *looked at him/turned toward*

frowned *darkly/slightly*

frowned in *concentration/confusion/evident concern*

frowned in her direction, but she pretended not to notice

frowned *too/while he listened to her*

frowned, and a small 'V' formed between his brows

frowned, deepening the lines about his mouth

frowning *in puzzlement/with concern*

he frowned *bewilderedly/not looking at all convinced*

his brow furrowed in irritation

his brows *converged in a/drawing into a puzzled* frown

his mouth was pressed into a frown

looked up at him, frowning

met her frown

stared at *whoever*, a puzzled frown between his *whatever color* brows

the frown creasing his brow

10

FACE

~

Face/Expression/Countenance:

aghast / alarmed / angry / anguished / baffled / bearded / bemushed / bitter / blanched / blushed / brightened / concerned / confused / contented / contorted / defiant / determined / delighted / distressed / dubious / excited / flamed / flushed / fumed / glared / grave / grim / grimaced / handsome / haunted / impassive / inscrutable / irritated / pained / peaceful / pensive / regretful / scowled / scruffy / shadowed / shuttered / skeptical / sobering / softened / stern / stony / stricken / sweating / tender / tight-lipped / tightened / tormented / unreadable / wary

a baffled/bemused expression on her face

a certain knowing filled his countenance

a cold look of determination on his face

a curious expression on her face

a day-old shadow of a beard across his lower face

a faraway look/all her uncertainty was/odd expression on her face

a flush stole across her face

a hurt look on her face which she quickly masked

a knowing look *swept over his/of extreme distress on the child's* face

a look of *delightful surprise on her face/feigned innocence*

a look of *misery/peace came over/shadowed* his face

a look of regret passed over him

a pained expression came over his face

a *pained look/peacefulness* crossed her face
a picture of peace and contentment
a scarlet flush cascaded over her features
a scowl *firmly in place/on his face*
a scowl marred his *face/features*
a scruffy beard
a stricken look *crossed/washed over* her face
a thundercloud descended over his face
a *worried furrow replaced her smile/worry line creased her brow*
admiration shone on his face
alarm flashed briefly over her soft features
all color drained *from/out of* her face
all humor left his face
an *almost snide expression passed over his face/expressionless stare*
an excited gleam filled her face as she looked up at him
an expression of *skepticism/terror* on his face
an icy *aloofness/glare*
anguish *clear on/lined* her face
anxiety written into their strained expressions
anxious lines furrowing his face
astonished expression
bearded face grim with concentration
beheld her stricken face
beneath his hungry gaze
black disapproval on his face
blood *drained from her face*
breaking off at the look on her face
brings a smirk to his face
cheeks bristled with a day's worth of beard
cheeks warmed *under his gaze/with the compliment*

cheeks were flushed with pleasure and excitement

color was rapidly returning to her face

concern lining his face

confusion *flit across her features/reflected in her gaze*

confusion *scudded about/skittered across* her face

controlled her facial features and

could read the concern in his expression

couldn't resist staring at her face, surrounded by unruly curls

countenance as open and friendly as

cruelty etched his features

curiosity on their faces

darkly handsome face arrogant

deep *crimson stained her face/lines etched his face*

desperate to ease the pain on her face

displeasure *crossed/written all over* his face

dread drained the blood from her face

everything showed in his face

expression *a mix of pain and anger/begged him to understand/ clouded with disappointment/didn't change/filled with hunger/ grew serious/grew taut and forbidding/holding a hint of regret/ just as disgruntled as hers/melted into a look so pained/mirrored his deadly intent*

expression of *incredulity/stunned disbelief*

expression turned wary

face *a mask of anguish and fear/alight with joy/as pale as parchment/ashen in color/became serious as he shook his head/ betrayed nothing of her feelings/bleached of color/broke into a broad grin/buried in her hands/burning with embarrassment/ closed up tight/clouded with thought/contorted in sorrow/ contorted in terror/controlled and impassive/crimson with mirth/crinkled into a wreath of smiles/dark with concern drawn and worried/devoid of expression/drained of color/etched with deep concern/flooded with embarrassment/flushed and eyes bright/flushed hotly/flushed with exertion/ghastly pale/*

glistened with excitement/grimaced in pain/had gone white as death/half in shadow/held regret/is creased with worry/lit up with childish delight/ kept morphing into/lit with pleasure as she/looked hard and dangerous looked thin and drawn/marred with concern/mask of worry/marked by peace/mottled with bruises was grim/open and kind/plastered into a scowl/ravaged with grief/revealed nothing/ruddy from the wind/set in expectation of a reprimand shining with eagerness/shown with compassion/shrouded in mistrust/steeped in shadow/storm of anger/streaked with tears/stricken with fear/taut with resentment/tear-streaked/transfigured by hope/turned livid with rage/warm with embarrassment/went hard

face contorted with *pain/hatred/terror*

face full of *concern/genuine compassion/hope*

face *glowered* with *anger/rage*

face held an expression of deep concentration

face lined with *concern/fatigue*

face shining with beads of sweat

face shone, full of life

face twisted with *anger/pain/rage*

face was *cast in deep shadow/etched with concern/lined with age/rigid with control*

face was *grim/hard,* his expression almost angry

face was horribly swollen and streaked with blood

face was pale, eyes wide with terror

face/countenance/features full of *anguish/pain*

faces beset with *urgency/fear*

fatigue and confusion on her face

features *grew harsh/had softened/set in disapproval/tensed in a frown/twisted in anguish/were tense with irritation*

felt her face *flame/go hot* with embarrassment

felt *her face heat/the breeze touch his cheek*

felt sorry for her when he saw her face

felt the blood *drain from/rush to* her face

flashes of doubt crossed her lovely features

framed her face with his hands, the two of them lost in each other

from the look on *the man's/whoever's* face, something had happened

frost-kissed cheeks

greeted him at the door, her lined face warm with welcome

had a terrified look on her face

hand soft on his face

he *scratched his stubbled/held her hand against his* cheek

her face a study of pure, blissful peace

her face *alive with hostile suspicion/lifted to the sun*

her face as pale as the white linen pillow behind her

her face *filmed with sweat and ghostly pale/paling suddenly*

her face *lit up and her eyes sparkled/was flushed from running*

her face *quivering with indignation/set with determination*

her face *told him he had been correct/was bright with discovery*

her features *paled/were wrought with worry*

her pert nose wrinkled in distaste

her visage glowed with health

hid her face against

his ancient face was weathered

his countenance *contorted/stony*

his craggy face broke into a scowl

his expression *betrayed nothing/had stiffened/thunderous/turned solemn/turning wary/was grave*

his expression one of determination and intensity

his face darkened, and a look of unutterable suffering clouded his blue eyes

his face hardened *into chiseled lines/still more*

his face *looming less than a handspan away/unreadable*

his face muscles clenched at her words

his face obscured by a thick, golden beard

his face was *anguished/grim*
his features once more an unreadable mask
his features *pinched/shuttered*
his features *raw with grief/tensed and hardened*
humor flickered across his face
innocent/narrow face
large, bulbous nose
lifted her face to the wind, relishing its moist caress
nose had obviously been broken more than once
not a muscle moved in the hard planes of his face
pasting a false smile on *his/her* face
pushed his glasses to the bridge of his nose
put her hands over her face and wept like a baby
raised her face toward him and looked into her eyes
ravaged, desperate face
reached out to touch her cheek, but she slapped his hand away
said with a mischievous grin in his *eyes/face*
saw his muscles strain, his neck cord
shadow crossed her face
shadowed his face
splashed cold water on her face
staid expression
stood, white-faced and frozen, her hands covering her mouth
stroked her cheek thoughtfully
strong cheekbones
the lines of his face relaxed
the look of hope and relief on *his/her* face
the look of outraged determination on her face
the look on his face *revealed his skepticism/held concern*
the old man's face darkened
the sternness in his face melted when he saw her

the thought of slapping his face flitted through her mind

the *weariness in her face/weary expression on his face*

their faces *aglow with excitement/beset with urgency*

their leathered faces lined with trouble

then his face softened

threatening look upon his face

tilted her face *to/toward* the sun

time had driven that sweet innocence from her face

time had ravaged his face

tried to mask *his/her* surprise

tried to read *his/her* face

trying to keep a straight face

turned *a stunned face toward/her face up to him*

turned to face him, his expression suddenly serious

turns her face to the moonlight so he can see her more clearly

ugly face

unable to face the censure on his face

unbidden, her face flashed through his mind

undisguised hatred on his face

vulnerability flashed across her face

was looking up into his face

weary face

weathered *face/features* fraught with distress

whole face lit up

worry *and concern etched his face/began gnawing away at her/ etched across her face*

A. Lips/Mouth

~

a *baffled/bemused* expression twisting his lips

a big hand clamped over her mouth

a grimace twisted his lips

a hand snaked out to clamp tightly over her mouth

a tremble quivered her lips

anger flashed across his face, but it was quickly replaced with a tight-lipped smile

blood trickled from the corner of his mouth

bitterness etched the set of his mouth

caught her bottom lip between her teeth

curled his upper lip in distaste

clamped his teeth together and forced himself to keep his eyes on her face

expression of abhorrence that curled his lips

features brightened as a broad grin spread across her face

full *firm mouth/mouth curving into a smile*

ground his teeth in frustration

her mock frown said more than her words

her mouth had a stern, self-important set to it

her mouth moved in response, but no words came *out/forth*

her mouth moved to deny his words, but no sound came out

her mouth opened and closed like a salmon poached from *whatever water*

her mouth *snapped shut/trembled at the corners/was wide and full*

his lips had formed a rigid line, and the muscles in his jaw throbbed

impudent quirk of her lips

lip curled in disgust

lips bled where she bit them to keep from screaming

lips *compressed into a tight line/formed a thin white line of suppressed anger*

lips *curled/curling cynically/into a smile*

lips *curved in a lopsided grin/lifted into a bitter smile/parted in surprise/pressed together/pulled into a hard smile* lips parted as if to speak, but no sound came forth

lips skimmed tenderly over hers

lips *slightly/softly* parted in wonder

lips *teased/trembled*

lips thinned to a compressed white line of fury

lips twitched with *a grin/amused approval*

mouth became a grim line of determination

mouth *blooming into a smile/curled upward/felt as dry as dust/had gone dry/started to water*

mouth *compressed for an instant/curving into a wistful smile*

mouth descended on hers, hard at first, but instantly softening to warm, soft, teasing

mouth *fell/gaping* open in horror

mouth set in a *firm/hard* line

mouth was dry, his brow sweating

pursed *his/her* lips *and then grinned/thoughtfully*

pursed/pursing his/her lips

saw *it in the set of his mouth/the surprise on her face*

smiled through tight lips

the lines carved around *his/her* mouth and *his/her* haunted eyes

wiping the blood from his lip, his eyes glaring furiously at her

B. Chin/Jaw

~

a chin so strong

a hard, square cut jaw

agony twisted his features, his jaw set hard

chin high, eyes flashing

chin jutted proudly as she refused to answer his questions

chin *lifted stubbornly/rose defiantly*

chin *quivering/trembled/rose a notch/started to quiver*

clenched and unclenched his jaw several times

didn't miss the leap of muscle along his jaw for a fleeting second before the smile appeared

from the set of his jaw

her chin jutted forward as she squared her shoulders and sat up straight

her chin *rose as he closed in/went up and her eyes blazed with fire*

jaw *clenched/dropped/set/throbbed/tightened*

jaw *dropped open in shock/locked in anger/was set grimly*

muscular line of his jaw

rubbed his chin and thought about it

took her chin in his hand and tilted her face upward

wiping his chin with

worked the muscles in his jaw

C. Brows

~

arched a *dark/single/sly* brow expectantly

arched *an eyebrow at her/her eyebrows slightly*

brow *creasing in thought/darkened threateningly*

brow furrowed in deep concentration

brow furrowed *in question/over eyes that held concern*

brow furrowed with *doubt/worry*

brow furrowed, lost in thought

brow *quirked as he/rose*

brows *dipped ever so slightly/drew together/knit into an expression of*

brows knit together *as he narrowed his eyes/in thought*

brows knitted *in confusion/into a deep frown*

bushy eyebrows

cocked a dubious brow at him

cocks an eyebrow, questioning

concern *knit his brows/stitching her brow*

eyebrows *arched up/were raised in frank surprise*

his dark brows drew together

his eyebrows *raised in query/rose in shock*

D. Forehead

~

a cold sweat breaking across his forehead

creases in his forehead deepened

forehead *creased with genuine concern/glistened with a faint layer of perspiration/took on a troubled wrinkle/wrinkled in a frown*

11

BLUSH

~

a blush *fired her cheeks/heated her face*

a blush stole over her pale skin

accepted her blush in answer

beneath his regard she could feel herself blushing

blush heightened

blushed *a fine pink/and turned away/crimson*

blushed and lowered her eyes

blushed *charmingly/delightfully/hotly/prettily/uncomfortably*

caused a rush of heat to her face

cheek flamed with red

cheeks gradually took on color as she

color *bloomed roses/heightened* in her cheeks

color *in her fine-boned/washed over her* cheeks

felt her cheeks grow warm *with embarrassment/as she studied his handsome face*

felt her color deepen

felt her face *flame/flush* with embarrassment

felt the color that raced from her throat to her cheeks

felt the heat rise up his neck and spread across his cheeks

flush in her cheeks deepened

had the grace to blush

heat *flamed/rushed* her *cheeks/face*

heat infused her face

heat scorched/heightened color in her cheeks

her cheeks *crimson/flamed*

her cheeks *flushing at the thought/pink with delight*

her cheeks grew warm as she remembered the

her color heightened

her delicate cheeks flushed the color of the roses she so loved

her face *burning with humiliation/flamed as she saw*

prayed she wasn't blushing

turned her head away before he could see the tell-tale blush no doubt spreading across her face

12

EYES

aggrieved / agonized / alighted / amused / assessed / avoided / beady / beckoned(ing) / bitter / blinked / bored / bright / burned challenged / closed / cold / compassionate / concerned / danced(ing) / darkened / deadly / determined / dimmed / disbelieving / downcast / enormous / enquired / excited / expectant / fierce / flashed / flickered / furious / gazed / glanced / glared / glazed / gleamed / glimmered(ing) / happy / hooded / horrified / icy / intense / interested / invited(ing) / kind / merry /

moistened / murderous / narrowed / open / pained / penetrated queried / questioned / remorseful / rolled / sad / scornful / searched / sharpened / shifted / smoldered / softened / somnolent sparkled / stared / stormy / thoughtful / triumphant / troubled / turbulent / twinkled(ing) / unseeing / warmed / warned(ing) / wary / watched / watchful / watered / wet / widened / wild

a depth of compassion in her eyes that was unsettling

a determined fire lit her eyes

a flicker of amusement lighted his eyes

a *gleam/glimmer* of deviltry *touched/stole into* his eyes

a glint of understanding entered his dark eyes

a hint of warning in her eyes

a mere flicker of his eyes and *whoever* moved

a *merry twinkle/sadness* in his eyes

a sinister gleam of satisfaction/affection glimmering in his eyes

after a *grueling glance from/mental rolling of her eyes, she*

alarm *filled/flickered in* her eyes

alert eyes taking in all around him without appearing to

allowed her eyes to stay locked on his

allowing his eyes to slide languidly down her length

an appreciative twinkle in his eyes

an invitation in her eyes

as he lifted his eyes, she read an unmistakable hunger there

as he watched her go

as she glanced around

asked softly, his dark eyes questioning her

at him, demanding an answer with her eyes

at his simple words her eyes filled with tears

avoiding his *eyes/gaze*

avoids *her eyes/looking at her*

aware of the sideways glances

beady/beckoning eyes

before her fascinated eyes

bent slightly at the knees to meet *his/her* gaze

bitterness and hurt/emotion surged into his eyes

blast/damn his *cursed hide/eyes*

blinked *and rubbed her eyes/away the vision*

blinked back *another wave of tears/the dampness in her eyes*

blinked her *whirling/reeling* thoughts away

blinked *his eyes in rapid succession/to stem the tears in her eyes*

blinked them back (tears)

blinking *rapidly/the sting of disappointment from her eyes*

blinking up at him with those huge *blue/brown/green/hazel/whatever color* eyes

brown/blue/green/amber/whatever color eyes probed hers

brown/blue/green/whatever color eyes *clouded/sober/blazing*

brown/whatever color eyes filled with amusement

brown/whatever color eyes regarded him shrewdly again

brushed a windblown strand of hair out of her eyes

cast a *look toward/sidelong glance at/an uneasy glance around*

cast down her eyes, but a smile played at the corner of her mouth

cast her *an intense look/gaze down with a blush*

cast *him/her* a withering glare

cast wary glances at

catching and holding her gaze

caught her eye *while she/with a wink*

chuckled, his eyes dancing with life

closed her eyes *against a powerful wave of desire/in distress*

closed her eyes and *leaned into his kiss/struggled to suppress*

closed her eyes, fighting to draw air into her lungs

closed his eyes and *ceded himself to sleep/drew a slow, steady breath/succumbed to the weariness*

closed *his/her* eyes, but the horror of what *he'd/she'd* seen wouldn't be erased so easily cold *blue/whatever color* eyes, as chilling as

cold eyes were deadly

compassion filled her eyes

concern darkened his eyes

concerned *gaze/look* in her eyes

contemplated *him/her*

could bear no more hurt in those sad, pale eyes

could look at her forever

could see by the steely glaze in his eyes that he wouldn't be convinced

could see *how fervently she meant it/the guilt in his eyes*

could see in her eyes how painful it was for her

could see the *indecision in her eyes/sadness in his eyes/shock on her face*

couldn't meet his eyes

cut a dark, irritated gaze at her

cut her with a steely look

dabbed her fingers at the corner of her eyes

dangerous currents glittered in her eyes

dared *him with her eyes/not look at*

dark amusement lit his eyes

dark eyes *blazing/meeting hers warmly/wide*

dark eyes searched her face as if he would read her mind

dark *gaze swept over/startling eyes*

dark hair and flashing eyes

darted a look at

dashing her hand beneath her damp eyes

desire darkened his eyes

determination turning his eyes to steel

did she know her eyes held an invitation?

didn't even try to wipe away the tears

didn't like the look in his eyes when he said it

didn't miss the spark of displeasure in his eyes

distress shown in her eyes

dragged her eyes from

emotions warring in her eyes

empty eyes

enfolding before her eyes

ever his eyes watch you

expression *closed and hard/didn't change/mirrored his deadly intent/of tenderness in her eyes/one of loathing*

expression *fierce/hardened/inscrutable/stony/tight-lipped/unforgiving*

expression turned almost cruel as he sneered

expressive *blue/whatever color* eyes

eyed each other warily

eyed *him/her appraisingly/coldly/defiantly/expectantly/suspiciously/sympathetically/thoughtfully*

eyed *him/her* with *distant disfavor/frank appraisal/with wariness*

eyed the woman closely

eyed/eyes him suspiciously

eyeing *him/her* with disfavor

eyelashes were wet with tears

eyelids grew heavy

eyes a deep *azure/warm brown/whatever color*

eyes a steely reflection of some yesteryear

eyes *alighted on/beamed with approval/began to mist/beseeched hers/betray her/betrayed no emotion/big and fearful/blazing hotly/blinded by tears/boldly raking her/brightened with anticipation/bulged with greed/caught her briefly/filled with compassion/full of hope*

eyes *as cold as the blade of his sword/assessing him boldly*

eyes began to blur as her body grew weak

eyes blue like the cloudless sky above her

eyes bore *into hers/through*

eyes bore into *him/her* with accusation

eyes bright with *exhilaration/teasing*

eyes *bright/brightened* and *expectant/merry*

eyes *brimmed/brimming* with *secret humor/tears*

eyes burned *into hers/with resentment*

eyes closed *against the shadow of the night/as though he were in pain*

eyes clouded with *defeat/tenderness and warmth*

eyes cold *and deadly/with disdain*

eyes crinkled *at the corners/with his broad smile*

eyes crinkly as she smiled

eyes *dampened/stinging* with tears

eyes danced and twinkled in the firelight

eyes *danced/dancing* with *humor/mirth*

eyes dark and *somber/stormy*

eyes dark with *desire/need*

eyes darkened, and his thick *whatever color* brows drew down

eyes *darted/darting everywhere/back and forth*

eyes drawn to her protruding belly

eyes feasted hungrily on her

eyes filled with *admiration/yearning/menace/shadows/wild rage*

eyes filled with tears that threatened to spill over on her cheeks

eyes filled with *understanding and she nodded/unspoken anguish/torment/distress*

eyes fixed dreamily on the dancing flames

eyes fixed her with a fierce look

eyes fixed on *him/her* in challenge

eyes flared wide *with alarm/and angry*

eyes flashed *dangerously/defiantly* as

eyes flashed *fire/with anger*

eyes flashed with *a sudden intensity/fury as she looked back at him*

eyes *flashing with urgency/flew open/flickered with hope/fogged with desire*

eyes flew to *his face/him*

eyes focused on some unseen person or place

eyes full of *apologies/concern/confusion and pain/secrets*

eyes gleaming with appreciation

eyes glinted *merrily/with tears*

eyes glinting with the *challenge/threat*

eyes *glinting/glistened* with *delight/glee/mischief*

eyes glittered with deadly rage as

eyes glossed over with grief

eyes glowed softly

eyes grew distant, far off yesterdays alive again

eyes grew *flinty hard/more serious/serious*

eyes grew serious, but his smile remained

eyes had grown soft and thoughtful

eyes *half shut in thought/hard on hers/heavy lidded*

eyes held a hurt so raw he had to look away

eyes held a *knowing look/resolve she hadn't seen there before*

eyes held *his/hers*, questioning

eyes held the slightest flicker of hope

eyes holding the promise of vengeance

eyes hot and stormy with anger

eyes immediately scanning his surroundings

eyes *implored him/locked with his/sparkling with mischief*

eyes intent on her face

eyes lifted slowly, finally landing on

eyes linger on her

eyes lit *for battle/up with excitement/with humor*

eyes locked *on each other/with hers in silent challenge*

eyes looked *deep into hers/hard and unflinching*

eyes looked deep into *his/hers* as she watched him

eyes *looked hard/mesmerized by him/narrowed/narrowed to slits*

eyes looked hurt, like a cornered animal

eyes looked to have absorbed more pain than

eyes luminous with hate

eyes *met hers with a simple understanding/misty with tears*

eyes moved over her with contempt

eyes *narrow/narrowed assessingly/with fury*

eyes narrowed in *a flash of fury/anger/irritation/speculation*

eyes narrowed to *dangerous/sullen* slits

eyes narrowed with *amusement/suspicion*

eyes narrowing *as he stares down/to contemplate her*

eyes *never leaving/penetrated/pinned/probed* hers

eyes *opened wide/turned into slits*

eyes pooled with *tears/fresh tears*

eyes puffy from lack of sleep

eyes raged with fire

eyes rapt with interest

eyes *reflected/reflecting what she was feeling/wry amusement*

eyes remained *dark with concern/glued to her mouth*

eyes revealing for one unguarded moment the yearning in his soul

eyes *rolling back in her head/rounded with surprise/scrunched up tight/searched the darkness/searching hers/shifted to/shone with alarm/shot daggers at/snapped with fury as/sought out/sprang open/steady as they fell on/still held a slight doubt/stung from lack of sleep/sunk in his head/swam with tears/swimming with emotion*

eyes said what his words didn't

eyes seemed suddenly to shoot sparks

eyes shown *happily/with sympathy*

eyes shown with a trust he didn't take for granted

eyes shown with *admiration/disapproval*

eyes slid down her length, hot and hungry

eyes slowly *opened/took in the*

eyes so filled with trust that he could barely breathe

eyes softened at the admission

eyes *sparkled/sparkling* with *amusement/fury/with the challenge*

eyes spoke volumes about how much he cared for her

eyes *taking in/thinned to slits*

eyes that stared back at her with guarded apprehension

eyes *told her he disapproved of/turned serious*

eyes *twinkled/twinkling* mischievously

eyes *warm/warm with compassion/went wide with shock*

eyes welled with *relief/tears and she shrugged/unwelcome* tears

eyes welled, but she didn't give in to tears

eyes were *a caress/enormous as she looked at him/pools of pain/still swollen*

eyes were *alive with color/arctic cold/blazing/concerned/ dilated with pain/filled with undeniable hatred/hard and angry/ incredibly dark/intense and sober/large and long-lashed/sunken in dark circles/warm and possessive/wide with shock/wistful for a moment*

eyes were as hard as the blade of a sword

eyes were bright with *excitement/passion*

eyes were cold, expressionless

eyes were on her face, intent, searching

eyes were on him now, watchful

eyes were red, her *cheeks/face* tear stained

eyes were wide with *fear/terror*

eyes wide and *full of innocence/mocking*

eyes wide *in sheer delight/with new concern*

eyes wide with *anticipation/fright/hurt*

eyes widened for the barest moment

eyes widened in *feigned/genuine* shock

eyes widened in surprise and awe

eyes widened like a startled deer staring down the headlights of an on-coming truck

eyes, blue as the seas

feeling his eyes on her

felt he was looking straight through her and saw everything

felt *his eyes widen/the heat of his eyes*

felt the familiar sadness gather in her eyes

feverish eyes rimmed with the dark circles of chronic ill health

finally broke eye contact

fire *blazed/kindled* in her eyes once more

fixed her gaze on

flashed *a quick look in his direction/him a glare*

flashed her a *look of disapproval/thunderous look*

flushed under his boldly admiring stare

followed her *aunt's/sister's/friend's* gaze to

followed her *gaze to/wary gaze*

found his eyes drawn to her

found *whoever* standing in the hallway, her back against the wall, eyes closed

from the moment I first laid eyes on you

fury blazing in his dark eyes

gave her a *black/considering/murderous/quelling* look

gave her a *cursory once over/droll look/long level look/long-suffering roll of her eyes*

gave him *a puzzled glance/an enquiring look*

gaze *bold/came up to his/fixed/rested on/wandered*

gazed at her with grateful eyes

gazed at him like an adoring schoolgirl

gazed *helplessly/solemnly* at

gazed thoughtfully across

gazed up at *whatever*

gazes locked in a silent battle of wills

gazing up at her haggard face

gentleness he saw in her eyes

glance *as cold as polar ice/fell on*

glanced about as if to ensure nobody was within earshot

glanced around the empty room

glanced around to find herself the object of everyone's avid attention

glanced at *him/her uneasily/with sympathy*

glanced at *him/her*, surprised by *his/her* offer

glanced away for a long moment

glanced *in apology/nervously at/worriedly toward*

glanced over *his/her* shoulder

glanced sidelong at *him/her*

glanced toward *him/her* as *he/she* shrugged

glanced, woe-stricken

glare stalled any further objections

glared at her *in anger/silently*

glared at the *man/woman* in silent challenge

gleam of triumph in his eyes

glorious vision

glowered across the table

got a look of terror in his eyes

gray/hazel/whatever color eyes were as dark as the storm

had *a mischievous/that faraway* look in her eyes

hadn't been able to take his eyes from her despite his best intentions

hard eyes and an arrogant manner

hard gaze narrowed

hard *glare/stare bore down on/boring into her*

hatred burned bright in his eyes

haunted eyes stared back at him

he looked into her eyes, her lovely *whatever color* eyes

he quietly observed her, his eyes dark and unreadable

he scratched his head, his eyes narrowing in concentration

he shook his head, his eyes shining behind his wire-rimmed glasses

he towered over them, his eyes never leaving their faces

he/she all but rolled her eyes

he/she sighed, rubbing at *his/her* eyes

heaven is in your eyes

held *his/her* eyes with an unwavering gaze

her anguished heart reflecting in her eyes

her brown eyes like rich pools of melted chocolate

her eyes and heart so open

her eyes burned and her vision was blurred

her eyes *crinkled when she smiled/widened disingenuously*

her eyes fell to his mouth

her eyes looked huge and pleading

her eyes *said she understood/snapped*

her eyes *searched his face/were direct and searching*

her eyes told him not to make promises he didn't mean

her eyes were red and swollen, her voice thick

her gaze lifted to his

her sorrowful eyes, pleading with him to

her terrified eyes, darting this way and that, caught sight of

her *whatever color* eyes *alight with mischief/twinkling*

hid her anxious thoughts as she dropped her eyes to

his cold, bitter eyes

his dark *condemning gaze/eyes snapping/gaze holding hers/possessive gaze*

his expression *darkened/thoughtful*

his expression filled with scorn

his eyes *alight with mischief/assessed her body/bitter*

his eyes and his face as cold as a January storma concerned look came into his dark eyes

his eyes and voice serious

his eyes assessed the fields they'd *plowed/cleared*

his eyes *bored/burned* into hers as he returned her stare

his eyes closed against the shadows of the coming night

his eyes closed, glazing over

his eyes *commanded hers/darkened in a blaze of heat*

his eyes cut to *whomever*, scalding him with his look

his eyes dark *and smoldering/with torment*

his eyes darted toward the top of the staircase

his eyes *delved into her/devoured her as she walked toward the/disturbingly intense/drinking her in/fixed on mine/gleamed with mischief/gleamed with purpose/glittering anew with anger/growing fierce/huge in his face/narrowed to cold slits/never revealed his feelings/promised vengeance/questioned her as she/raked over her/ remained hard upon hers as/searching hers/shot daggers at/sparked with interest/were stormy/wide with worry*

his eyes *growing/getting* accustomed to the darkness

his eyes *lingered over face and figure/narrowed and pinned her where she stood*

his eyes *never wavered from her as/but an inch away from hers*

his eyes *on her white face/roving over her body*

his eyes shifted *meaningfully/of their own volition* to

his eyes tender, yet ablaze with desire

his eyes were *clear and direct/teasing*

his eyes were cold, his mouth curved in a sneer

his fingers gentle on her jaw as he tilted her head up to look into his eyes

his gaze *remained fixed on/warm on hers*

his gaze roved over her from the top of her upswept hair down to her slippered toes

his hooded eyes narrowed

his hungry eyes coursed down her naked body

his penetrating gaze held hers

his shrewd old eyes watched as

his *whatever color* eyes *settled on/mocking*

his/her agitation shone only in *his/her* eyes

his/her eyes *bespoke sorrow/darting from/drifting shut/glazed with desire*

his/her eyes lost in *his/hers*

his/her eyes meeting *his/hers* squarely

his/her steady gaze revealed nothing

his/her worried gaze fixed on

hoped he couldn't see the tears in her eyes

horrified at what *he/she* saw

huge anxious eyes

hungry stare

I know you're scared. *Whoever* gets the same look in his eyes when he's worried about me

I've seen the doubt in your eyes

icy/intense blue/whatever color eyes were riveted on her

if *he/she* closed *his/her* eyes *he/she* could *imagine/still remember*

ignoring the warning sparks in *his/her* eyes

immediate disappointment clouded her eyes

imperious/intimidating stare

in a blur of tears she

interest gleaming in his eyes

keeping her *eyes lowered/gaze averted*
kept her eyes downcast
kept her *warm brown/whatever color* eyes focused on him
kept *his/her gaze downcast/eyes trained on*
kind and soulful blue eyes
knew his eyes were on her
laid long-suffering eyes on him
lashes *fluttered/long and sensuous*
leaking at the eyes
leaned close to hold her gaze
leaned his head back and closed his eyes
let herself get lost in his eyes
let his eyes drift shut, absorbing the peace
let his eyes *drift to/linger*
let his gaze roam over the comfortably familiar room
let his gaze *slide/travel* appreciatively over her
let/letting his eyes *drink their fill/roam over her*
leveled a *cold/dark quelling look/murderous* gaze at *him/her/them*
leveled a steady bead on the man
leveled an *assessing/impatient* look at
leveled her gaze at *him/her*
lifted a heavy eyebrow
lifted her chin, meeting his eyes
lifting *his head to pin his eyes on her/hungry eyes to*
lighting the depths of his eyes
locked eyes with the aggressor
long lashed dark brown eyes
long sweeping lashes
look at me. Just me
look at me. You won't have to find out

look grew serious

look in her eyes would haunt him for eternity

look of *horror/revulsion* on her face

look of *shock conveyed/promised retribution/sympathy he sent her*

look *puzzled suddenly/was incredulous*

look would have wilted a less stronger character than

look. He's no' dead

looked *abashed/admiringly at/about the house wistfully/aghast/annoyed/appalled/at ease/almost wistful/relaxed*

looked after him with a troubled expression on her face

looked and sounded like a petulant child

looked *annoyed at the suggestion/anything but convinced*

looked around *in a nervous manner/the room nervously*

looked around, breathless with excitement

looked as *black/dark* as a storm cloud

looked as if he longed to hit her and it was taking all his strength not to

looked as if she wanted to say something more, but remained silent

looked as if she were counting to ten before speaking again

looked *as sad as he'd ever seen her/at her bitterly*

looked at each other and looked away

looked at her and grinned

looked at her *closely/crossly/curiously/directly/furiously/grimly/searchingly/strangely*

looked at her *from beneath hooded eyes/glowing face*

looked at her in *amazement/disbelief/surprise*

looked at her with *a questioning glance/interest/tenderness/those steely eyes/wide, terrified eyes*

looked at her with total *admiration/adoration*

looked at him *blankly/expectantly/for support/hopefully/in confusion/miserably/oddly/solemnly/wistfully* looked at him in *puzzlement/surprise*

looked at him long and hard, then nodded

looked at him through *bleary/weary* eyes

looked at him with a *teasing expression/twinkle in her eye*

looked at him with *concerned eyes/eyes full of mischief/ unmistakable pride in his eyes/wounded eyes*

looked at him with cool, *whatever color* eyes

looked at him with *raw hatred/unbridled fury* in his eyes

looked *at him with stricken eyes/back with uncertainty/ bewilderedly at/big and solid/chagrined/challengingly at/ concerned/confused for a moment/considerably displeased/ considerably taken aback/daggers at him/decidedly uncomfortable/deeply contrite/desperately frightened/engrossed in/pensively at her*

looked at him with the practiced, critical eye of a bartender

looked at him without a shred of compassion

looked at him, *not sure what to say/startled*

looked at *him/her apologetically/for support/speculatively/ thoughtfully*

looked at *him/her* with a *sad smile/hard eyes*

looked away *briefly/guiltily*

looked away, *feeling her cheeks burn/shutting out his gaze*

looked away, unwilling for him to see her unhappiness

looked away, *wanting/hoping* to protect *his/her* heart

looked confused *and bewildered/but eager*

looked deeply into his eyes, imploring him

looked *devastated/grief-stricken/disoriented/despondent/ displeased/distracted/doubtful/dumbfounded*

looked down at her feet, words failing her

looked down at her, peace stealing around his heart

looked down at them with twinkling eyes

looked down in bewilderment and then a shockwave went through her looked down, breathing in deeply

looked everywhere but at *home/the grocery store/the mall/wherever/whoever*

looked *exasperated/exhausted/exquisite/fit to kill/frightened/genuinely panicked/haggard/him fully in the face/horrified/huge/hurt by his outburst/incensed/increasingly annoyed/instantly disapproving/menacing/nervous and pale/old and beaten/panicked/peaceful/pleased/radiant/relaxed and happy/satisfied/serene/shaken/skeptical annoyed/smug/so fragile/startled/stricken/strained and exhausted/stunned by/wary/wistful/woebegone/worried*

looked *exceedingly pleased by the prospect/faintly amused as*

looked expectantly *at/in his direction*

looked for the *chieftain/jarl/president/whoever*. There was no sign of him

looked hard at what mattered most to him

looked her over with a warm appraising look

looked *him fully in the face and/hurt*

looked incredibly comfortable with him

looked into *her eyes and saw raw pain/the distance*

looked into his warm, loving eyes

looked intrigued *at the prospect/with her*

looked lifeless. I was afraid he was already gone

looked like he might consider murdering her

looked more *bored than annoyed/furious by the minute*

looked on *horrified/with amusement as*

looked on with dull, hopeless eyes

looked out into the night thoughtfully and then back at him again

looked outraged at the indiscretion

looked *pensive as he considered it/puzzled for a moment*

looked pensive, *his/her* mind clearly drifting elsewhere

looked searchingly at

looked shocked at being dismissed

looked *so endearing/taken aback/thoroughly agitated*

looked *stunned/uncomfortable* when she said it

looked through tear-brushed lashes

looked to her *mother/father* for guidance

looked to him, then let her gaze travel to the back of the room

looked to *him/her* for answers

looked to the distant horizon

looked toward wherever, his expression pensive

looked *unconcerned as/unhappily at*

looked uneasily up and down the hallway

looked up and met his *close/waiting* look

looked up at him and smiled, and he felt something he'd never felt before

looked up at him *expectantly/pointedly/silently/through sodden lashes/wearily*

looked up at him, *a flicker of dread in her eyes/her expression contrite*

looked up at *whoever* and blew out a slow breath

looked up from the *whatever*, blinked as though coming out of a trance

looked up *into his smoldering gaze/startled*

looked up with *a start/haunted eyes/interest*

looked *vaguely amused/vulnerable and frail/worriedly at/young and frightened*

looked visibly *disappointed/sick*

looking *admiringly at/apologetically at/around the table/at her intently/crestfallen/enraged/for his destiny/uncertain like a waif/plenty sassy/tenderly at her/up at him sadly*

looking anywhere but at her

looking at her with unmistakable tenderness

looking at him through red-rimmed eyes

looking at *him/her/them* with *expectant faces/renewed interest/sudden tenderness* looking completely unconcerned about

looking *daggers/dismayed* at

looking faintly *embarrassed/worried*

looking for the very best in everyone he meets

looking furtively around the room

looking into *her astonished eyes/his steady gaze*

looking into her eyes with firm patience

looks like you've let a charmed life. Looks can be deceiving

lovely eyes huge and wary

lowered her eyes as quickly as she raised them

lowered/lowering her *gaze/lashes*

made her look at him again

made her nervous. He could see it in her eyes

made his eyes go cold and narrow

made the mistake of gazing into his eyes

make cow eyes at him

meaningful glance

meets/met his/her eyes

met her *accusing gaze/gaze levelly/husband's eyes/pitying gaze*

met his *any color* eyes

met his brother's worried expression with one of calm confidence

met his eyes cooly

met his eyes, then jutted her chin in the air

met his *fixed stare/gaze evenly/*gaze *levelly/squarely/ unflinchingly/with her chin lifted*

met his *furious/harsh* gaze with

met his gaze with a calm she didn't feel

met his *mocking/questioning/smoldering/tender* gaze

met his *steady look/wrinkled eyes*

met the question in his eyes

mischievous twinkle in his eyes

misery and hopelessness/murder in *his/her* eyes
narrowed *his/her* eyes, watching *him/her* intently
narrowed *his/her* gaze *at him/in curiosity*
narrowed/narrowing his/her eyes *in accusation/with loathing*
no obvious checking him out, just an up-down flick of the eyes
nodded miserably, blinking the moisture from her eyes
noted the look of alarm in her eyes
observed the hurt in her eyes
open your eyes and I'll be here waiting
opened her eyes *and met his watchful gaze/with a heavy effort*
opened his *bleary eyes/eyes lazily*
opening her eyes with an effort
panic filled her eyes
paused and met his eyes
penetrating eyes
pierced her with *a sharp look/an icy glare*
piercing *blue/whatever color* eyes remained fixed on her
pinned her with *a deadly/an icy* stare
pinned her with a gaze that was dark and penetrating
pinned her with a *menacing glare/steely gaze*
pinned her with his darkest glower
pinned *him/her* with a baleful glance
pinning her with *an icy stare/a purposeful gaze*
pinning his intense *blue/whatever color* eyes on her face
pity in his eyes
predatory eyes followed her everywhere
pretending his eyes were tired so he could secretly wipe away a tear
profound puzzlement in his eyes
quickly cast a downward glance at
raised feverish eyes to *him/her*

raised her *face toward him and looked into her eyes/gaze to his*

raised *his eyes wearily to the skies/remorseful eyes*

read *it/the reluctance* in her eyes

recognized the threat in his eyes

red, swollen eyes

red-rimmed eyes bore evidence

refused *the tears stinging the corners of her eyes/to meet his eyes*

regret in his gaze

relief *filled/flashed through* her eyes

reluctantly he lifted his gaze from the creamy mounds

rendering her eyes a deeper

returned his gaze

rolled *his/her* eyes heavenward

rosy cheeks highlighted lively *hazel/whatever color* eyes under tufted *gray/whatever color* brows

rubbed a hand over *his/her* tired eyes

rubbed his fingers across his eyes and sighed

rubbed *his/her* eyes, bone weary

rubbed the fatigue from *his/her* eyes

rubbed weary fingers over *his/her* eyes

sad eyes

saddened to see

said as tears filled her eyes again

said with a mischievous grin in his *eyes/face*

salt spray stinging her eyes

sat back, closed his eyes and released a slow breath

satisfaction in his eyes

saw a flash of disappointment in *his/her* eyes

saw *a storm raging/abject misery* in *his/her* eyes

saw alarm piercing her eyes

saw her *glance toward/startled look*

saw *honesty reflected/hope dawning* in her eyes
saw immeasurable pain
saw the *concern/conflicting emotions* in his eyes
saw the *confusion swirling/pain mirrored* in *his/her* eyes
saw the dark pain lancing *his/her* eyes
saw the *stark frustration/unmistakable glint of* determination in *his/her* eyes
searched *his/her* eyes, but couldn't read *his/her* thoughts
searing gaze
seeing her *dazed expression/lying there/made him tremble*
seeing her tremble, he braced her elbow with his hand
seeing the look in his eyes hurt him deeply
sent him an agonized glance
set all-knowing eyes on her
set cold, *blue/whatever color* eyes on her face
shaded *his/her* eyes with *his/her* hand
shaded *his/her* eyes, squinting into the distance
shadow *concealing his eyes/fell across her*
shame in her eyes
sharp, impassive eyes
she entwined her fingers around his neck and gazed into his eyes
she looked up, an unreadable expression *in her eyes/on her face*
she met his eyes, and his heart lurched
she swallowed hard, her eyes misting over
shielded her eyes against the sun
shifty *and staring eyes/eyes and a cold heart*
shook his head as he opened his eyes
shot *an angry look in her direction/her a steady look*
shot *him/her/himself a murderous/an exasperated* look
sighed and glanced around
sight of her was arresting

slanted a look at her, the amusement in his eyes a contrast to his solemn tone

slanted *her a puzzled look/him an enquiring glance*

smiled coldly, his eyes raking over her

smiled, *his/her* eyes still concerned

smoldering *hatred/passion* in *his/her* eyes

smudges of exhaustion under her eyes

solemn *brown/blue/green/any color* eyes

something flickered in *his gaze before his eyes lifted back to her face/the depth of his eyes*

something hard and cold shimmered in their depths

something *sinister/wild and dangerous* in his eyes

sorrow in her eyes

spared a distracted glance at

spat, his eyes dark with fury

speech failed her as her eyes darted to his lips

squeezing her eyes shut, she shook her head violently

stared *after/at* him, *mouth agape/his expression pensive*

stared at her a long time as if thinking about it

stared at her in *disbelief/surprise* and then smiled

stared at her like he was willing her to understand

stared at her *searchingly/with a knowing gaze/with hate flashing in her eyes*

stared at him a moment in suspicion

stared at him *cooly/expectantly/helplessly/speechless/warily*

stared at him in *confusion/disbelief*, eyes wide with shock

stared at him in shock, her mouth hanging open

stared at him *open-mouthed/uncomprehendingly/wordlessly*

stared at him with hope in her eyes

stared at him with open *disdain/hatred*

stared at him with troubled *whatever color* eyes

stared at him, *completely unnerved/horror chilling the blood in her veins/seething*

stared at *him/her* in disbelief

stared at the empty doorway

stared *at their entwined hands/coldly at her/down at her hands into the dancing fire/dubiously at/in open disapproval/pensively into space/wistfully at/without blinking*

stared down at her, his lips a grim line

stared *him down and his grin faded/in wide-eyed horror at*

stared *mutely at him/tenderly upon/unseeingly at*

stared out at *whatever*, the past clearly weighing on her

stared suspiciously at *whoever*, his eyes hooded like a hawk

stared *up at him with undisguised hatred/with undisguised contempt at*

stared up into the raging storm of his *whatever color* eyes

stared, unable to take her gaze from him

stared/staring levelly/bleakly at

staring *after her in consternation/down at her with adoration*

staring at *her cards with cool aplomb/him with open defiance/ the back he presented to her/the glowing embers*

staring back with wary, hooded eyes

stealing surreptitious glances at

stony look of determination in his eyes

stormy gray eyes

studied her *closely/face intently*

studied *her for a moment and gave a firm nod/the stiff line of her back*

studied her hands, avoiding his eyes

studied her *through narrowed eyes/ through the candlelight/ under half closed eyelids/with a hint of doubt in his gaze*

studied him with shrewd *blue/whatever color* eyes

studied *him/her* closely

studied *him/her* for a moment, and sighed

studied his friend and silently disagreed

studied his *impassive face/profile*

studied *whoever*, a twinkle lurking in his eyes

studies her before replying

studying *him/her* with concerned eyes

surprise *in her/registered in his* eyes

suspicion burning in her eyes

tears filled her eyes and she blinked them back

tears *glistened/shimmered* in her eyes

tears *rimming/stung* her eyes

terrible truth in his eyes

thanked *him/her* with *his/her* eyes

the anxious lines bracketing his eyes and mouth

the *appeal/devotion/fear* in *his/her* eyes

the *blue/whatever* color of his eyes darkened, intensified

the bluest eyes she'd ever seen

the cold savagery in his eyes

the dark shadows under his eyes

the defeated look in her eyes

the determined glint in his eyes

the eyebrows dropped low over *gun-metal gray/whatever color* eyes

the fathomless depths of *his/her* eyes

the fight was gone from her eyes

the first sign of hope softened her eyes

the flash in her eyes

the fringe of thick black lashes which rimed her *chocolate-colored/whatever colored* eyes

the frustration in his eyes was palpable

the furious look in his eyes as he

the genuine concern reflected in his eyes threatened to

the glance he shot her was scathing

the gleam *intensified in/hatred radiating from* his eyes

the hard look in his narrowed eyes

the *heartbreak/hopelessness* in *his/her* eyes

the hues of his eyes changed with his moods

the life was already gone from his eyes

the light died in her eyes

the light *in his eyes flickered and died/brought a chill down her spine/went out in her eyes*

the light you've kindled in my son's eyes

the lines around the eyes and mouth were deeper, but her skin was still soft and smooth

the longing in *his/her* eyes

the look in his eyes melted her in a single heartbeat

the look in *his/her* eyes gave *him/her* pause

the look in *his/her* eyes told *him/her* everything

the look she speared him with was anything but calm

the lure of those *gray/whatever color* eyes fascinated him as nothing else ever had

the men's *eyes met and clashed/gazes drew to*

the *mischievous spark/miserable look* in *his/her* eyes

the mists of confusion cleared from his eyes

the moisture in his *eyes/gaze* clouded his vision

the most impossible *whatever color* eyes

the most pleasing sight my aging eyeballs ever beheld

the *naked anguish and fear in her eyes/pain in her eyes was terrible*

the pain in her sapphire gaze said she spoke the truth

the *panic in her eyes began to fade/pride in his eyes warmed her down to her toes*

the sadness he'd seen in her eyes haunted him *as he/long after he departed* the sadness in her eyes was almost enough to make him change his mind

the slightest sense of alarm filled her eyes

the soft look in her eyes

the sparkle had disappeared from her eyes

the sparkle in his *midnight blue/whatever color* eyes held her captive

the stars in her eyes had blinded her to the truth

the *storms raging/tender regard* in *his/her* eyes

the terror in her eyes was stark

the tight set of his lips, the dangerous gleam in his eyes

the tiny lines around her eyes crinkling in amusement

the *veiled depths of her/wonder in his* eyes

the wildness in his eyes frightened her

the worry in *his/her* eyes *faded away/is obvious*

the wounded look in her eyes nearly breaking his heart

their eyes *locked in a battle of wills/touched briefly*

their eyes *meeting over/met and held/met over the crowd*

there was pain and uncertainty in her eyes

they double glared each other

though tears welled in her eyes, there wasn't one ounce of weakness in her stance

threw him a dark look

tight set of his lips, the dangerous gleam in his eyes

too observant eyes

took a long, thoughtful look

torment flashed in his *whatever color* eyes

tossed a worried glance at

trapped in his eyes

tugging at her heart and stinging her eyes

turmoil darkened his eyes

turned around and found herself gazing up into his eyes

turned away but he could see the tears in her eyes

turned back, his eyes unreadable

turned from his disturbing *golden-brown/whatever color* eyes slanted a glance at him

turned *her watery gaze to/wild eyes on*

turned *his gaze to her and smiled/loving eyes toward her husband*

twinkle of mischief came into his eyes

unable to *meet his gaze/peal his eyes from/take his eyes from her*

unbridled hate flared in his eyes

uncertain gaze

uninvited tears welled in her eyes

vivid *blue/whatever color* eyes

wanted to *savor seeing you walk out of here for the last time/see desire in her eyes*

wariness in *his/her* eyes

wariness shadowed *his/her* eyes

warm *brown/gold/amber/whatever color* eyes

warm, loving eyes he'd grown so accustomed to loving

wary eyes sought her

was engulfed by the intense look of longing in *his/her* eyes

was that suspicion in his eyes

watched *a shower of sparks/angrily*

watched as his wife caught her breath and struggled vainly to control her hysteria

watched her *every move with hawk-like intensity/like a hungry predator*

watched her *from the corner of his eye/hips sway/in cold silence/ stiff withdrawal from the room/walk to the door/with a knowing expression in his eyes*

watched her, his eyes narrow and hard

watched him *curiously/set the logs on the dying embers*

watched him *for so long he shifted in his chair/weave his charm* watched him through heavy eyes, fatigue screaming through every muscle

watched him with *mild curiosity/wary eyes*

watched him, speechless

watched *him/her* in silence

watched his *son with wonder/son's face closely as he said the words*

watched in *amazement/disbelief/wonder*

watched in *sickened/stunned* silence as *he/she*

watched the *flames together/last bit of color drain from her face/muscle flex along his jaw/play of emotions on her face*

watched the *golden plover/whatever bird* wing its way out of sight

watched the *parade of feelings flit across her face/unfolding scene with dismay*

watched with *rapt fascination/relief as*

watched, missing nothing

watching *her every move/him through half closed eyes/his muscles flex/with dark hooded eyes*

whatever color eyes *alight with excitement/flashing*

whatever color eyes gentle as he smoothed hair from her face

whatever color eyes *sparkling/twinkling/warm* with amusement

when she finally looked up his heart caught at the anguish he saw in her eyes

when she smiled, her eyes didn't light up

whirled around, eyes flashing

white light filled her eyes

wide *brown/whatever color* eyes searching for his approval

wide, terrified eyes

willing away the tears that stung at her eyes

willing *himself/herself* to meet *his/her blue/dark* eyes

winked *and grinned/at his gape-jawed friends*

wiped *discreetly at her eyes/her eyes on her sleeve*

wiping the moisture from her eyes

wistful expression *crossed her face/in her eyes/look in her eyes*

wistful *look/yearning in her eyes*

with a triumphant glint in his eyes

with an air of expectancy and delight shining in her eyes

with an impatient jerk of her hand she wiped the moisture from her eyes

with *bewildered/haunted* eyes

with moist eyes and a quivering lip

with solemn *blue/whatever color* eyes

without looking, *he/she* could see the disappointment in *his/her* eyes

worry swirling in his eyes

wouldn't meet his eyes

yet did his eyes remain shadowed by concern

you know he has eyes on us now

your eyes always tell the truth

13

SLEEPING

a sleepy, peaceful place

after a sleepless night

as he held her in his arms, she fell asleep

as she fell asleep she was smiling

as the fog of sleep cleared from her brain

breathing had deepened to the slow rhythm of sleep

broken and restless sleep

closed her eyes and feigned sleep

collapsed *in an exhausted stupor/into a fretful sleep/in bed* consumed with his feelings for *whoever,* he got little sleep that night

despite a fitful night of little sleep

dozed fitfully

drifted off to sleep snuggled up next to

drifting *between sleep and wakefulness/in and out of a hazy sleep*

dull-witted from lack of sleep

during her hours of fitful sleeping on the sofa

eyelids *drooped/heavy with exhaustion*

eyelids grew heavy as the stress of the day overtook her

eyes dark and slumberous

falling into a fitful sleep

fast asleep *beneath his mindful eye/sprawled across the bed*

fell asleep, curled trustingly in his arms, a small, satisfied smile curving her lips

fell into *an exhausted sleep/the sleep of exhaustion*

gazed at his sleeping face

giving in to her exhaustion, she

go back to sleep. There's no sense in us both being awake

got too much on my mind. I can't sleep

had likely been abed for hours

had taken a long time to fall asleep

he dozed and tossed through the night

he quit the room, eager to find his bed

her hair *a wild mess from sleep/unbound for sleeping*

her *sleep-heavy/solemn dark* eyes

his eyelids closing, surrendering to the temptation of sleep

his eyes highlighted by dark shadows from too many sleepless nights

his/her face gaunt, *his/her* eyes shadowed from lack of sleep

I wouldn't sleep at all tonight. I don't intend to

kept any hope of sleep at bay

maintained a pretense of sleep
murmured *in her sleep/sleepily/something in her sleep*
over the long, sleepless hours of the night he
paced her room restlessly, unable to sleep
rubbed the sleep from *his/her* eyes
said as she went back to sleep
said sleepily
settled herself between the *blankets/furs*
she didn't sleep, but lay in torment
she fell asleep, curled trustingly in his arms
sleep *began to pull at her/came fitfully to her that night*
sleep *eluded her/was elusive*
sleep was proving impossible
slept fitfully despite the wariness that plagued her body
slept soundly
snoring/snored softly
stared at his back as his breathing fell into the deep and even rhythm of sleep
stirred from sleep before daybreak
the music lulled her to sleep
then she drifted, exhausted, into sleep
too excited to sleep
tossed and turned until at last she fell into a fitful sleep
tried to lull him to sleep
try as he might, sleep eluded him
trying to forget the demons that wouldn't let her sleep at night
voice *still/was* thick with sleep
was already asleep
was asleep almost the moment her head hit the pillow
went to sleep before her head hit the pillow
within seconds, the man was in the arms of Morpheus

wouldn't be able to sleep an

you didn't get any more sleep than I did last night, did you?

14

ROMANCE

Hugging ~ Touching ~Kissing ~ Love ~ Lovemaking ~ Afterglow

A. Romance

*~

a *deep longing in his eyes/glance passed* between

a pang *of longing so sharp/of jealousy*

a wave of longing went through her

acutely aware of his nearness

awareness *of him seemed to escalate by the minute/simmered in her veins*

brushed a finger over her lower lip

budding romance

but her heart would not still

caught his tender expression on her

couldn't suffer the thought of her in another's arms

cradled her *gently/head in his palms and lowered his mouth to her waiting lips*

cradled his head between her hands, luxuriating in the thickness of his hair

didn't miss his smoldering glance

drew her as close as propriety allowed

drew in a *trembling/tremulous* breath

enclosed within his warmth

enfolded her in both arms

eyes rose to meet hers and her breathing suspended in anticipation

gathered her *into his arms/on his lap/tight against him*

gathered him up for a hug

gaze softened as it traveled down to fix on her mouth

had the feeling he could very well drown in the depth of her eyes if he lingered too long

had to remind herself to breathe

hand moved of its own volition to his cheek

hands itched to tangle in the glorious *curls/smoothness/softness/waves* of her hair

he chuckled, the pleasantly male sound wound its way through her, found a place somewhere inside her chest

he wanted to bolt—he'd never been up for the heart to heart stuff

he was finding it much too easy to stay in step with the pretty *red-head/whoever*

he'd been known to flirt some just to make life interesting

he'd been too proud to ever spill his guts about how he felt about her. But *whoever* had been the one. The one that got away

he'd never imagined he'd find himself attracted to a woman who wanted nothing more than to wish him to the devil

heart ached in places he'd assumed had atrophied long ago

heart pounding with such yearning he could almost taste her soft, moist lips on his

heart *suddenly in his throat/swelled with longing*

her beauty aroused his deepest passions

her body was weightless, boneless, moving with the natural rhythm of the sea

her chin lifted. They stood so close, instant awareness shot through her. The breadth of his shoulders, the heat of his big body reaching toward her

her *gentle strength stirred his lonely heart/heart filled with trepidation*

her warmth and softness heightened his awareness of her

her world had unraveled

his fingers curled around her neck. Rough-skinned but gentle. She couldn't have resisted him if she'd tried

his gaze lingered over her, a fathomless pool of unspoken things between them. Desires and promises. Curiosities left unsatisfied

his gaze settled over her mouth. 'A thousand times I've thought about it'

his glance vaguely troubled, held onto hers. Dark and smoldering, thickly fringed, his eyes had the power to make her forget *wherever they were*

his movements made her feel rocked by the ocean's waves. Over and over, the swells built, each threatening to wash over her and drown her completely

his scent filled her, saddle leather, and sweat, and damn it, it didn't matter he was

his touch, the exquisite simplicity of it, its tenderness and caring, delved inward and stroked something deep, something buried, something she was afraid to feel

holding her *close, he breathed in her scent/gently against his side*

how *do I stop my heart from wanting?/had she slipped past his defenses*

I can't remember the last time I felt like this. I don't think I've ever felt like this

I have feelings for her. I want to explore them

I want to do everything—and nothing—together with you

I want to *open my heart to you/share all my sunrises with you*

I want you to marry me. To sleep with me. To wake up next to me each morning

I'll make all your dreams come true. Mine already have

idly stroked her hair

image of her in his arms was never far from his thoughts

imagining her in another man's arms

insides clenched with yearning

isn't it obvious I have very deep feelings for you

isn't prepared for the tender feelings her new husband arouses

it was all he could do to keep from touching her

jealousy reared inside him

jolting her heart to new heights

large hand touched her with tender care

let his gaze slide appreciatively over

longed *desperately to hold her, comfort her, cherish her/to scoop her up in his embrace*

looked deeply into her eyes, willing himself not to sink into the depths of them

looked down at her trembling, full mouth and gently followed the curve of her lower lip with his thumb

lost in the warmth *and comfort of him, she/of his embrace*

loving gaze never leaving his face

B. Kissing

*~

a forbidden kiss soon makes

a kiss that *had fired his blood/spoke of a lifetime*

a quick and gentle kiss that he followed with a smile

absorbed in the wild abandon of their kiss, he

another *deep, drugging kiss/kiss followed*

as their lips parted, he whispered

been soundly kissed

began to shower her with kisses

being kissed senseless

bending his head to place a soft, chaste kiss on her mouth

bent *down and kissed her gently/to press a kiss*

broke off the kiss on a groan

broke off the kiss, her breath coming in short gasps

brought his mouth to hers with a hunger he couldn't hide

brushed *her lips with a brief kiss/his thumb across her lips in a whispering soft caress* caught her mouth with his, devoured it in a long, desperate kiss

claimed her *lips in a punishing kiss/mouth and took the kiss she'd offered*

claiming her *mouth with his/soft lips in a kiss*

coaxing her to meet his kiss

could still feel her lips tingling from his kiss

crushed his lips to hers

crushing her mouth hard beneath his

cut off her words of protest by kissing her

deepened the kiss as her hands slid up around his neck, her fingers caressing his nape

demanding *lips/thrust of his tongue*

drew her *into his arms and silenced her with a long, demanding kiss/mouth down for another kiss*

dropped a careless kiss on

emboldened, she slipped her arms around his neck and tentatively touched her tongue to his, delighting in the velvety feel

ended the kiss, but tightened the embrace

exchanging sweet words and even sweeter kisses

feasted on her mouth with unquenchable hunger

fingers twined in her hair, he kissed her hard, possessively

fought an urge to kiss her

gathered her in his arms and kissed her long and thoroughly

gave her a *kiss on her soft, wrinkled cheek/last quick kiss*

gave him a kiss on his leathery cheek

greeted her *pleasantly/with a kiss*

he closed his eyes, lost in the sensation of her mouth beneath his

he *grinned and bent to kiss her/groaned against her mouth*

he kissed her and pulled away from her. What's wrong? You act like a stranger

he'd never kissed a woman like her before and the urge to hold on tight and savor the moment damn near swept him away he'd wanted to kiss her for a long while now and wasn't a bit sorry for his actions

her blood began to heat as his skilled tongue slid across her lips slowly and sensually

her hand sliding up his arm did nothing to soothe the ache he had to hold her again and to feel her lips under his, opening to him, giving him free rein to fully taste the sweetness of her mouth

her *kisses were as hungry as his/lips were kiss-swollen*

his head lowered and hers tilted back

his lips *followed/met hers, the kiss lingered/touched her bruised cheek*

his lips moved over hers with exquisitely slow tenderness, teasing her with feathery kisses and tiny nibbles until she moaned softly

his mouth *closed over hers in a fervent kiss/enticed*

I'd sooner turn into a toad

kiss *as gentle as the brush of a feather/confused her senses*

kiss *said even more than his words ever could/took her by surprise*

kissed her *again, slower than before/briefly, his lips barely touching hers*

kissed her cheek, her neck, the base of her throat

kissed her *fondly/forehead/hungrily and hard/into silence/long and deep/so tenderly/soundly/until she moaned/very gently/warmly/with hunger*

kissed her like there was nothing he wanted more in this life than to have his mouth *locked on/pressed against* hers

kissed her softly, looking toward the sky

kissed her, *and this time she answered it with a need of her own/drawing the strength from her/stirring the passion between them*

kisses grew deeper, taking on a sense of urgency and branding her flesh and searing her conscience

kisses politely stolen (under mistletoe)

laid a chaste kiss on her cheek

leaned *in and softly kissed her cheek/over the hospital bed bars and kissed her*

lifted her *fingers to his lips and lightly kissed them/hand and pressed a kiss to her knuckles*

lifting her face to kiss him

lips *begging for a man's kiss/parted invitingly*

lips brushed against hers, gentle at first, then harder, deeper, with more urgency

lips hovered *a mere breath from hers/against her mouth*

lips *tasted of wine and promises of things to come/took hers in a hungry kiss*

lips *touched his/warm, unyielding*

lips were *every bit as soft and lush and yielding as he'd imagined them/warm, pressing gently on hers, yet firm*

lips were warm and firm, coaxing and teasing as he gently increased the pressure until her mouth opened of its own accord to invite him in

lost *himself to a kiss like he'd never experienced before/in sensation as his lips moved over hers*

lowered his head *and tasted/to kiss her*

lowered his head *to taste the nectar of/and captured* her lips

lowering his lips to hers for a gentle kiss

lying beside her, he rained light, quick kisses across her forehead and eyelids and down her cheek before nibbling lightly at her ear lobe

C. Love

~

a life filled with love—friends and family

a lot of people love you. Including me

a love *that was strong and sure/that's never going to end*

a woman with a sensible mind who doesn't look for romantic love but is willing to oblige me for

accept my gift. It is offered with love

all the love and goodness

an extension of their love to be nurtured and developed

and more than that, we've got love. Love will get us through this

and undying love returns

brought love to my life

can fill hearts with a love so strong it will endure forever

can you open your heart and love me again?

can't fall back in love with you, because I never fell out of love with you

cast lovesick eyes upon him

caught the woman he loved close

could be assured their love would weather the storm that lay just beyond the horizon

could see the love in her eyes

could she have actually fallen in love with this man

do you still love me?

do you think I love you less for *whatever happened*

do you want to be right and alone? Or bend a little and be with the love of your life?

does love you. I saw that in her eyes when

don't want to fall in love—not with you, not with anyone

eyes alight with love

eyes warmed with love

Father had never loved her as he should have, never shown her the affection she so desperately craved

felt a corresponding tug on her heart

felt the overwhelming love of her family

felt the pain of separation from their loved ones

filled with love for

found not only love, but peace

gazed into her love's glassy eyes and desperately pleaded with him to stay with her (not die)

God help him, he loved her

going to love you through hell or high water

had taught her about love

have a second chance at love. At life

have heart my love

he ached to tell her he loved her

he doesn't love you the way I do. He never will

he was in love with her and she knew *whoever* had feelings for him. Once they both figured it out, she had no doubt

heart filled with the love she felt for him

heart melted with love for

her heart crying out her love, even as her lips refused to give it voice

her love constant and unfailing

his *love/need* for her grew as the days *went by/wore on*

hopelessly and forever in love with you

how am I going to *forgive her/live without her/do whatever*? Love and patience, I guess

how it feels to know someone loves you with every ounce of their being—and then to learn it was all a lie

I blamed her–the person that loved me more than anyone in the world

I don't doubt that you love me

I don't want to fall in love—not with you, not with anyone

I know I love you

I know what it's like to hurt the people you love

I love and honor you

I love you just as you are

I love you more today than I did yesterday, and less than I will tomorrow

I love you so much. Only you. Forever

I love you, and I want to share my life with you

I love you, he longed to say. *Whatever*, he said instead

I love you. Don't ever doubt that

I love you. I didn't know what that meant. Didn't know what that felt like...until I met you

I love you. I don't care how long it takes you to believe it

I love you. I want you to remember that

I loved her you know. It was like nothing I've ever experienced

I need to know I'm the only woman you love

I promise *I'll/to* love you for the rest of *my/your* life

I trust you with my heart, my life, and my love

I'd fall in love again as I did then

I'll love you...always

I'm in love with her. It came over me before I knew it

I'm not going to stand by and watch the people I love get hurt

if I had never met you, I would have lived my life searching aimlessly for the one I was to love

if this is his time, he's going to be reunited with the woman he loves

if you love her so much, how could you let this happen

in the first bloom of love

insides melted at the love she saw shining in his eyes

it wasn't exactly a declaration of love, but it would do for now

it wouldn't be hard to love you

knew then and there if he hadn't loved her before, he loved her now

love and beauty. She loved her son so much that she wanted to make sure no harm would

love doesn't necessarily conquer all. But commitment does

love for her nearly overpowered him/has spoken to you in its own private way

love is a risk–but anything worth having is worth fighting for

love *is expressed in many ways/makes me stronger*

love is having someone to talk to. Someone you don't have to choose your words with

love is looking into someone's eyes and seeing yourself perfect for the first time in your life

love is *the most dangerous choice of all/unconditional and ageless*

love is when you have a bad day but then you see the one you love and everything seems to be okay

love *shining/shone* in his eyes as

love shone as bright as the afternoon sun

loved and revered by all

loved her *more than he dared/so much that he ached*

loved you every minute of every day–we just didn't say it or show it enough

D. Heart

~

ached / admired / beating / calmed / caught / cried / despaired / dreaded / empty / erratic / fluttered / hammered / hardened / heaved / hoped / joyful / leaden / leapt / loved / lurched / plummeted / pounded / pumped / quickened / raced / quickened raced / sad / sank / shielded / soared / softened / somersaulted / splintered / stopped / stuttered / surged / swelled / thudded / thumped / thundering / tight/ tugged / twisted / whispered / worried / wrenched

a dull pain in his heart

a familiar *pain pricking/pang wrenched his/her* heart

a fog of discontent settled on her heart

a fresh sadness grabbing her heart

a generous heart

a glimmer of hope dared to creep into her heart

a heart he'd thought safely secure, immune to the wiles of women

a heaviness settled over her heart

a moment of impending doom squeezed his heart

a sigh come from the recesses of her heart

a small glow of warmth wrapped itself around her heart

a *small/tiny* seed of *doubt/hope took/had taken* root in her heart

a strange fluttering of her heart

a tale of heart aching poignancy

a tugging sensation in his heart

across the stormy seas of her heart

all of it stayed heavy on her heart

allowed her dangerously near his heart

am the true home of your heart, and I know that

an *ache/empty feeling* in *his/her* heart

an unfamiliar tightness squeezed his heart

and yet, in *his/her* heart *he/she* knew it was true

angry despair brought fresh misery to *his/her* heart

angry despair welled in *his/her* heart

answer went straight to *his/her* heart

believed in *his/her* heart

bitterness welled in *his/her* heart

brought confusion to *his/her* heart

burning a painful hole in *his/her* heart

calmed *his/her* raging heart

caused *him/her* a lot of heartache

chilled *his/her* heart

cold dread lodged in *his/her* heart

comment set *his/her* heart pounding

compassion and admiration swirled through *his/her* heart

could he hear her thudding heart?

couldn't fail to move *his/her* battered and bruised heart

couldn't keep himself from touching her anymore than he could keep his heart from beating

couldn't stem the longing in *his/her* heart

courage in her soul and compassion in her heart

despite her efforts to shield her heart

despite *his/her* racing heart

did you not hear my heart crying out for you?

didn't anticipate how the family scene would assail the emptiness of *his/her* heart

don't let your head get in the way of your heart

dread filling *his/her* heart

drew back in alarm, her hand covering her racing heart

each piece of information had punctured a hole in *his/her* heart

emptied *his/her* heart

fear *gripped/seized* her heart as she raced toward

felt the words like a knife in *his/her* heart

found her heart and her home

had taken her heart *captive/with him*

has seen *his/her* share of heartache

has your heart softened a bit

he hardened his heart

hearing her pain was like a knife to his heart

heart ached for *him/her*

heart ached with a bitter sadness

heart aching for *his/her* pain

heart beat a rapid cadence

heart beat faster than the click of her high heeled *boots/shoes* on

heart beat out a hard and steady rhythm

heart beating madly in *his/her* chest

heart *began/beginning* to *hammer wildly/pound with dread*

heart caught

heart constricted with the thought of

heart *flew into her throat/flooded with warmth/gave a painful lurch/ gone eerily still/had to be healed /hammered a message/ heavy with grief/in her throat/leapt into his throat/heart leapt with hope/one quick thud/pounding in his chest/pounding within her/raced out of control/sang for joy as/sank heavily into her stomach/skipped a beat/ slammed against her chest/so full of love/suspended in his chest/swelled within her/threatened to explode in his chest/thrummed with anticipation/thumped in her chest/thundering against her ribs/took flight/twisted in pity/twisted into a Celtic knot*

heart *lurched oddly in his/nearly pounded out of her* chest

heart overflows with hatred

heart pounded *against/in* her chest

heart pounded *harder than before/with a mixture of fear and excitement*

heart pounded *in her chest/with fear*

heart *raced with anticipation/racing, shirt soaked*

heart seemed to have its own agenda

heart skipped a beat *as/when/at the sight of her*

heart skittered crazily in *his/her* chest

heart slammed *against her chest/into double-time*

heart swelled with *a mixture of happiness and grief/gratitude*

heart thudding hard against his chest

heart *thundered/thundering* in her *chest/ears*

heart torn into pieces

heart twisting with fierce protectiveness

heart was beating *faster than it should/very rapidly/violently*

heart was *behaving very oddly/in her eyes/racing dangerously/ thudding so loud she*

heart was in her throat and she struggled to find an answer

heart went out to *him/her*

heartache welled up inside *him/her*

heartbeat doubled

heartbeat *perceptibly quickened/quickening when she saw/ slowed as she remembered*

heavy of heart

her anguished whisper scored claws of grief across his heart her broken murmur tore at his heart

her gaze traveled the length of him, and her heartbeat quickened

her *hands wrapped around his heart/heart bade her to stay*

her heart *battling with regret and longing/beat a rapid staccato against her chest*

her heart *cried out/galloping wildly*

her heart *did a small, unexpected flutter/fluttered, as if disputing her silent objection*

her heart hammered *hard/wildly* against her chest

her heart heavy *as/with dread*

her heart *lifted at his words/lurched in her chest*

her heart no longer steeled for battle

her heart pounded *erratically/joyfully*

her heart *pumped at an alarming rate/raced at the thought*

her heart refused to process what her mind told her to be true

her heart *skipped a beat/slammed against her ribs*

her heart *skipped/skittered* at the sight of him

her heart stayed heavy

her heart stopped a beat as she gazed at his handsome features

her heart *threatened to break/thudded against her breast as*

her heart *thrilled at the mere thought of it/thrummed with anticipation*

her heart *urged her to pray, but/was already lost*

her heart whispered *liar*

her tearful *plea enough to break his heart/voice cutting him to the heart*

his hands went slack, and her heart burst at the anguish in his eyes

his heart *ached for her/caught in his throat/cold and empty/had hardened/in his throat/pounding against his ribs/pumped harder as/thudding at the sight of her*

his heart beat *faster with every step/out a warning*

his heart *missed a beat, then started to pound/sorrowed at her plight/suffered a twinge of sorrow* his heart *thudded to life/thundered in his chest*

his heartbeat *faltered/quickening*

his mind raced as fast as his heart

his voice stirred her heart

his words cut straight to her heart

his/her anguish tore at *his/her* heart

hope *blossomed/building* in her heart

hurried to him, *fear clutching/sounding at* her heart

if you break her heart, I just might have to break you

if you wrong her, I will tear out your heart

it *tugged at his heart as he said it/warmed his heart*

looked *at her in a way that melted/deep into her, all the way to* her heart

lost her heart to him

E. Emotions

*~

a confusing tangle of emotions

a myriad of emotions brewing on her heart shaped face

a series of emotions passed across his face

a surge of emotion welled up within him so powerful it choked off his breath

a sweep of emotion filled him

a swirl of emotions churned in her belly

a wave of confused emotions swept over her

a wellspring of emotions

after that emotional moment

aroused a mixture of emotion

awash in awkward emotion

been itching to settle the score since he'd been railroaded out of town

betrayal left scars that took a while to heal

betraying no emotion in his features

caught in a rush of emotions

choked off the words, overcome with emotion

choked with emotion

clearing his throat of emotion

closed her eyes, fighting for control of her emotions

concealed her emotions

concealing the unwelcome emotion

curbing his own emotions

daddy always hated it when I was emotional

doesn’t hide behind his emotions

emotion *choking her voice/clogged his*

emotion drew her throat tight and she couldn’t find the words

emotions got ahead of her/raw and close to the surface

emotions *in turmoil/ravaged by/reeled*

emotions remained a swirl of conflict and confusion

emotions rolled like a tumultuous thunderstorm inside his chest

eyed her without emotion

eyes bespoke her conflicting emotions

eyes were *emotionless/glistening with emotion/wide with surprise*

face *bore no/showed no signs of* emotion

feeling miserable and in sorry need of *having/feeling* his arms around her

felt a curious jolt of emotion

fighting off a rise of hopelessness

forced back her emotions

fought her emotions

gave in to the emotions that had been leashed for so long

gazed down at her, his chest tight with emotion

had an air of danger and mystery about him

had calmed herself enough to speak without letting her emotions show

had the ability to soothe her with the words she needed to hear

he demanded, driving his point home with cold precision

he filled her, this awful need in her which needed filling. He opened a part of her she'd closed up tight *however many* years ago

he would be her undoing or her salvation. She didn't know which

he'd poked at a raw spot he suspected had been gnawing at her a good long while

heart swelled with emotion as

her temples took on a dull ache; she needed coffee, hot and strong

hid his disdain. Swept aside his resentment and hate

his mouth worked with the emotions *he/she* was fighting to control

his voice gruff with emotion

hoped her face wouldn't give away her conflicting emotions

how dead her voice sounded—not only toneless, but emotionless

I hope people's fears don't overtake their emotions

in a rush of emotion and heartache

keep her emotions in check

knew better than to bring the subject up. She'd just get all hoity-toity as she tended to do sometimes

loyal, she learned in the short time she'd know him

F. Lovemaking

*~

a decade ago she'd been young and hot blooded. A firestorm in bed. Even now she made him hard from the remembrance

a moment of stillness hovered between them, as if he debated the everywhere he touched, tiny flames ignited until her entire body felt as though it were on fire

a slow burn of desire coiled through her

a sudden rush of desire

a wide, warm hand slid under her shirt, the other threaded up into her hair

all the desire he'd put on hold stormed him like a

allowing his weight to pin her against the *door/wall*

allowing lust to cloud his judgment

ample breasts

an hour or two of lovemaking would cure more than a couple of aches

and *for the next hour/with it the last of his restraint*

and then, at long last, breath suspended, she stared in fascination at that most secret part of him

arousal pressing intimately into her belly

as he *brought her to passion/readied her* again

as she *lowered herself down upon him/took the initiative*

as their bodies came together, she forgot any doubts she'd had

at last his fingers found the very core of her

awakening a hunger he'd kept buried for years

backside nestled against his loins

began a timeless rhythm

beset by a stab of arousal

between her thighs

big hands skimmed her hips

bodies spoke what words couldn't

bodies *united as one/were entwined*

body *ached/burning* with need

body *answered with a surge of need/hard and throbbing against hers*

body *responded/responding* with shameless intensity

body shuddered with the effort to control his passion

breast *filled his fingers/to chest, hips to hard thighs*

brought her to the brink of paradise

brushed the line of soft hair down the center of his stomach

buried deep inside you

but the heat in his body told him he'd better show restraint. He ended the kiss

calming the parts of his body that screamed at him to enclose her in his arms

caught in the crush of one embrace after another

chest anchored her beneath him

climbed onto the mattress and lay beside her

continued his way down to the swells of her breast

couldn't *completely control the stirring in his loins/stop himself by then*

crying out his name as she reached her crisis

cupped/cupping her *breasts/buttocks* and pressing her against the heat of him

denied himself release

desire *hot and rampant/overpowered him/pooled in her belly*

desire roared *through/throughout* him

down her belly, between her thighs

eager for all the delights he could teach her

eased *her down over him/up her skirts*

eased his arms around her and held her body against his

entered her, became part of her

entwined in each other's arms, they rocked

everywhere his fingers touched a warm trail of fire seemed to follow. Never had she felt the like

explored the delights of married love

eyes darkened as he rolled her over onto her back and straddled her, his hardened member once again probing her wet heat

eyes darkened in a blaze of heat

felt *heat rage through his loins/lust within him the instant he saw her*

felt his *arousal, hard and insistent/blood stir again*

felt the *evidence/length* of his desire

felt the *first stirrings in her loins/warm womanly curves of her body mold against him*

fiery passion took over

filled *her, relishing the heat of her tight sheath/*with the musky scent of their loving

filling her with his need

fingers *brushed her flesh/straying lower to caress her intimately*

fingers dangerously close to brushing her breasts which sent an oddly heated sensation to her belly

fingertips brushed the swell of her breasts

flames of desire

floated on waves of unfamiliar sensation

following with his own body

for one moment she felt something hard and long press against her thigh and then, suddenly, he shifted away from her

found he was an exceptional lover

gasped as his tongue thrust inside her mouth

gave herself over to the joy of their lovemaking

gently flicking the bud of her femininity

going to get my needs tended to

groaned in pleasure

groin tightened involuntarily

ground himself into her

had *enflamed his passion/loved her well*

hand curled around his neck instinctively and she could feel the steady beating of his heart against the side of her breast

hand *drifted to her breast, cupped it, squeezed it/was on her buttock*

hands *caressed/caressing* her *back/spine*

hands *going to the fall of his trousers/seeking to cover herself*

hands roved over her back and down, crushed in the folds of her skirts, clasped her buttocks hands skimmed over his upper arms, corded with muscle as he held himself off the bed

hands slid down to rest at her hips

hands unfastened the *strings/drawstring* to his pants

hard throbbing *shaft/of his manhood*

hardness straining the fabric of his trousers

he had loved her again

he lifted one stockinged foot and slowly rolled the stocking down

he stepped closer, a light shift of his body moving toward hers. Anticipation coiled through her, the knowledge of what he might do. The comfort he seemed to know she needed

he too exploded, emptying his seed deep within her with a loud *cry/shout*

heat woke in the depths of her body

held her gaze with smoldering passion in his eyes

her *body arching off the bed against his seeking mouth/ womanhood*

her body *entwined with his/quickly reawakened/surrendered*

her *body molded against his and he felt her* response/*every curve fitted to the hard planes of his body*

her *breasts rose and fell as she gasped for air/full, rounded breasts*

her most intimate and secret *parts/places*

her soft whimper mingled with his groans of pleasure

hips grinding into her

his body *on fire /said what he could not*

his *entire body thrummed with need/lustful intentions very clear*

his *fingers parted her nether curls/hand closed over a full, lush breast*

his hands *caressed her with slow insistence/wandered over her freely*

his jutting erection pressing against her belly

his maleness pressed against the juncture of her thighs

his masculine flesh ~ erection

his member *grew/sprang free*

his need heightening

his skin warm and smooth beneath her fingers

holding her body so intimately close to his, feeling the soft, satiny texture of her skin, and inhaling the scent of roses wafting from her hair ignited a fire in him

hot mouth closed over her

ignoring the sexual tension she felt building between them

intent to force himself on her

it was wrong to be with him this way, but she couldn't stop herself

it's not food I'm craving

joined with her

jolt of sensation made her gasp

just looking at her brought a familiar heat to his loins

just thinking *about her made him squirm in his chair/of those kisses stole her breath, turned her limbs to water*

kept her up most of the night with lovemaking

kindled his blood to new heat

kissing a path down to her intimate flesh

knew how to stir a man's blood

know it will take a long time before you feel about me the way I feel about you

laid her *gently on the bed/hand over the evidence of his desire*

leaned down and kissed her cheek while allowing his hand to brush across her breast

leaned forward, unwittingly affording him a tantalizing view of her cleavage

leaned into him, *drew in the scent of his warm skin beneath the robe and relaxed/rose up on her toes and*

left *a trail of kisses down her neck and shoulders/her body deliciously replete*

let me make you mine in truth

lips followed where his fingers had gone

looked down at the swell of soft skin above the bra cups

loosening her hair from its pins

lost *herself in the magic of their first night/in each other's arms*

lost track of how many times they had coupled

lust blazed in his eyes

lustful gleam lurked

G. Afterglow

*~

after they made love

afterward, drained of all her strength

as the fog of lust slowly dissipated

as they *floated in the aftermath of passion/lay in bed together afterwards*

awoke the next morning

basking in the warm afterglow of their lovemaking

body *lay curled against his chest and thighs/soft and warm against his*

completely spent and sated

in *passion's aftermath/the circle of her husband's* arms

later, so much later, when

lay *contented in his arms/entwined in the afterglow of their lovemaking*

lay in each other's arms, sated and *content/sleepy*

lay in the circle of his arm, her breathing even and peaceful

H. Romance Extras

*~

'twasn't the time or place for trysting

a *cry slid past her lips/look of undisguised passion*

a delicious thrill tightened her breasts

a flood of pleasure that claimed her breath, her body

a low growl came from deep in his throat, a sure sign he was losing control

a *sense of foreboding filled/shiver of anticipation rippled through* her

a *testament to his desire/throaty moan escaping her*

abrading her face with the shadow of his beard

ache for her to be near me

ached to *feel his arms around her/hold her in his arms*

all hope of resisting him vanished

amber eyes heavy with lust

amenable in the bedroom

an odd sensation filling her lower belly

and she was his

arched toward him

arm snaked around his neck

arms crept up and around his neck. She buried her fingers in the soft curls at his nape, glorying in his harsh groan

arms crushing her so firmly against him she could hardly breathe

arms *slid around his waist unbidden/were strong and held her close*

before *he gave in to raw desire/she could command her mutinous body to*

bent close to nuzzle the lobe of her ear

besotted with *him/her*

body felt deliciously alive, every nerve ending alert and attuned to him

body was hard and lean against her

breath *came harshly/rasped along his naked shoulder*

breathing *in her scent like a man starved/uneven and quick*

brushed his thumb across her lips in a whispering soft caress

by now he was so close

caressed the rock-hard plane of his jaw

caught her arm and pulled her against him, molding her body to his lean hard one

caught himself before he reached out to touch her cheek

cheeks *flamed with heat/flooded with fire/went up in flames*

combed his fingers through her untangled hair

control *slipped another notch/teetering*

could feel his breath, warm on her face

couldn't *give in to the longing for her/stop himself, he had to touch her*

crushed her to him with a groan

curves begged to be touched

cut a glance down at her

damn him for a rogue and a scoundrel

dark face hovering a scant inch from hers

desirably beddable

desire *ate away at/for her blinded* him

desire flickering in his eyes

desperate to calm her racing heart

didn't trust herself to stop him if

dredged up what little restraint he possessed

drew her into a full embrace

drowning her in sensation

entrapped his heart

enveloped her in a *fierce, hard hug/loving embrace*

eyes *dancing with devilry/darkened with passion/were heated with raw desire*

face cast in shadows

feeling the soft, satiny texture of her skin, and inhaling the scent of roses wafting from her hair ignited a fire in him

felt *alive with anticipation/disoriented as though she were lost in a swirling cloud* fingers *tangled in her hair and forced her gaze up to his/twined through hers*

forced last night's erotic images to the back of (*his/her*) mind

fought the tide of desire rising within him

frightened by the *depth/intensity* of her *reaction/response* to him

gave in to temptation and stroked a stray curl from her cheek

giggles were muffled beneath his demanding kiss

goal was to soothe and seduce her, not scare her more

gown coming to rest in a crumpled heap at her feet

groaned, answering his kiss

hand *caressed her neck/moved slowly*

hand *skimmed up over her back/sliding through her hair*

head on his chest, she heard his heartbeat, slow and even

heart slammed into his chest wall

heat *barreled through him/burned through her blouse, searing her*

heat *pooled/pooling* low in *his/her* belly

held his breath as she began to remove her linen gown

her *dainty pink tongue toyed with the corner of her mouth/parted lips beckoned him to kiss her*

her tongue came out to lick the moisture from her lips and he groaned

his gaze *came to rest on her mouth/caressed the gentle planes of her face*

his *hands shook with the need to touch her/larger hand lingered to cover hers*

his look of possessive jealousy

his name *lingered like a caress/was barely a whisper on her lips*

holding her fast as he drank from her lips

how had the woman grown so important to him

I *can't wait till we're alone/don't know what to do. That's all right. I do*

I just went up and looked at the baby. He's beautiful. Want to make another one?

I need time to think about it. Take as much time as you need. Yes. What? My answer is yes

I still have one good arm to love you with

if we don't stop now, I don't know if we'll be able to. Would that be such a bad thing?

if you're having second thoughts, now's the time to tell me

looked down at him through a wild tangle of hair

Add Your Own Tags!

*~

Add Your Own Tags!

*~

Thank you for chosing the Regency~Medieval Historical Phrase Book. I hope you will graciously consider leaving a review on your favorite book site.

ABOUT LEANNE BURROUGHS: The Breadth of the Audience: Readers who are fans of Diana Gabaldon, Julie Garwood, Philippa Gregory, Susan King, Johanna Lindsay, and Jean Plaidy will like Leanne Burroughs. She appeals to readers who are looking for historical accuracy with strong, believable characters—readers who want to be immersed in the period with well-rounded, memorable characters.

Add Your Own Tags!

~

Add Your Own Tags!

~

***Add Your Own Tags*!**

~

CPSIA information can be obtained
at www.ICGtesting.com
Printed in the USA
LVHW040316290420
654635LV00003B/230

9 781942 606215